Western Frontiersman Series
XVI

FRANÇOIS XAVIER AUBRY
From Tassé, *Les Canadiens,* II

François X. Aubry

Trader, Trailmaker and Voyageur in the Southwest

1846-1854

by

DONALD CHAPUT

Natural History Museum
Los Angeles

THE ARTHUR H. CLARK COMPANY
Glendale, California
1975

Copyright ©, 1975, by
THE ARTHUR H. CLARK COMPANY

LIBRARY OF CONGRESS CATALOG CARD NUMBER 74-27225
ISBN 0-87062-110-6

Contents

Illustrations

Foreword

When I became interested in Western exploration some years ago, I was puzzled by the lack of a biography on Aubry. The early French sketch by Tassé (1878) was excellent on some aspects of his career, but was weak when dealing with frontier personalities and geography. Ralph Bieber edited a few Aubry journals (1938) and prepared a fine brief biography, but never carried it further.

Aubry was no obscure petty trader on the frontier. From 1846 to 1854 he was the busiest, most effective merchant on the Saint Louis-Santa Fe-Chihuahua-California routes. His caravans were usually large, and his speed and reliability in getting the goods to the right market ahead of others was well known throughout the country. Along with this mercantile reputation he developed a talent for individual travel that has never been surpassed. His eight-hundred-mile trip on horseback from Santa Fe to Independence in five days is a record most likely to stand forever. Unsatisfied with the route found by earlier travelers, Aubry spent money and valuable time in finding short-cuts on the Santa Fe

and Chihuahua trails. When the United States government planned a series of surveys to find the best railroad route to the Pacific, Aubry, at great personal expense, made two overland trips from San Francisco to
Santa Fe. This route along the 35th Parallel was later
followed by the Santa Fe Railroad.

Although a few historians have mentioned some of
these events, they have entirely missed the man. Aubry
enjoyed, in fact, cultivated, national acclaim. But he
wanted his name also to be associated with the highest
personal characteristics. Honesty, bravery, reliability,
integrity – these and similar noble attributes were consistently assigned to Aubry by all who knew him.

There is no major collection of Aubry Papers, partly
because of his early, tragic death, but there are useful
scattered items in various libraries and archives. The
most fruitful have been the Huntington Library, San
Marino, California; Denver Public Library; and the
State Records Center, Santa Fe. From Quebec I have
received much help from Father Hermann Plante,
Séminaire St-Joseph, Trois-Rivières; Clément Plante,
St-Justin; and Raymond Gingras, Archives Nationales
du Québec.

My colleague Harry Kelsey read the manuscript and
provided many suggestions for research. Kathy Don-
ahue and Lowell Hebrandson of our Museum Library
were most helpful in locating unusual items on inter-
library loan. William Mason of the Museum staff
unraveled many geographical puzzlies. Mary Butler of
the staff aided by preparing copy for the maps.

No one knows the eastern California deserts better

than Dennis Casebier, and he has helped me trace Aubry's routes in detail. Others who have helped with research questions include Dr. Myra Ellen Jenkins of the State Records Center, Santa Fe; Lee Myers of Carlsbad, New Mexico; Lile Tuttle of Ulysses, Kansas; Father William Barnaby Faherty, S.J., Saint Louis University; and Dr. Gaston Tisdel, Laval University, Quebec.

Much of the thread of the Aubry story is held together by newspaper accounts. I am especially thankful to Mrs. Winifred Stufflebam of the State Historical Society of Missouri, Mrs. Frances Stadler of the Missouri Historical Society, and Ms. Stephany Eger of the Museum of New Mexico. Without the use of newspapers from those collections, little serious research could be done on mid-century Western history.

I have placed a few unusual sections in the Appendices. Aubry was on some trail most of the period from 1846 to 1854, so I have summarized in a Chronology all of his trips. In his travels from such varied parts as Missouri, New Mexico, Chihuahua, and California, Aubry encountered in more than a passing manner dozens of interesting frontier personalities. Brief sketches of many of these individuals have been gathered in a *Dramatis Personae* section. The Aubry California-New Mexico diaries have been published several times, but his journals of trips along the Santa Fe and Chihauhua trails have generally been unknown. I have included a selection of these journals.

Much of this book is concerned with the Santa Fe Trail. Recently four outstanding books have appeared on the Trail, and for years historians will be in debt to the authors: Louise Barry, *Beginning of the West;* Jack Rittenhouse, *The Santa Fe Trail: A Historical Bibliography;* Morris Taylor, *First Mail West: Stage Coach Lines on the Santa Fe Trail;* and Aaron Cohen, *The Santa Fe Trail: People and Places: A Catalogue of Books & Pamphlets.*

A research grant from the American Philosophical Society enabled me to make several fruitful trips, and the Museum in many ways made the research a rewarding experience. My wife Toni worked with me in every way, from research to final draft.

DONALD CHAPUT
Natural History Museum
Los Angeles

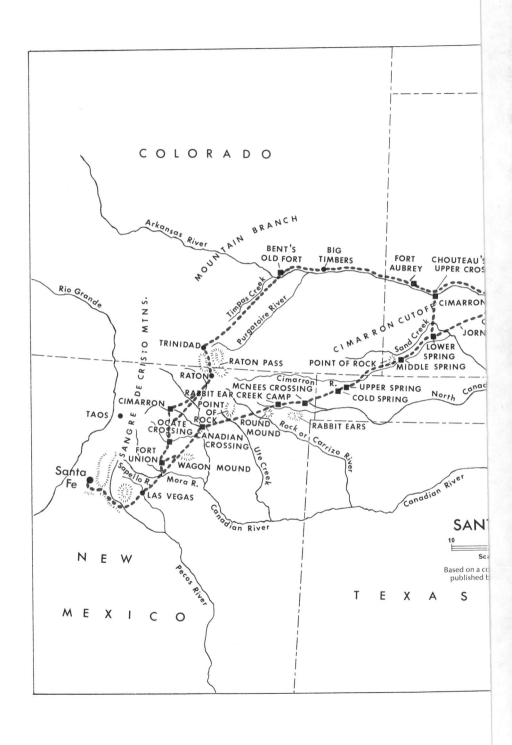

COLORADO

Arkansas River

MOUNTAIN BRANCH

Rio Grande

TimPas Creek

Purgatoire River

BENT'S
OLD FORT

BIG
TIMBERS

FORT
AUBREY

CHOUTEAU'S
UPPER CROS

CIMARRON

CIMARRON CUTOFF

JORN

TRINIDAD

RATON PASS

POINT OF ROCK

Sand Creek

LOWER
SPRING
MIDDLE SPRING

SANGRE DE CRISTO MTNS.

RATON

Cimarron

McNEES CROSSING

R.

UPPER SPRING

TAOS

CIMARRON

RABBIT EAR
CREEK CAMP

COLD SPRING

North Canad

POINT
OF
ROCK

ROUND
MOUND

Rock or Carrizo River

RABBIT EARS

OCATE
CROSSING

CANADIAN
CROSSING

FORT
UNION

WAGON MOUND

Ute Creek

Santa
Fe

Sapello R.

Mora R.

LAS VEGAS

Canadian River

Canadian River

SANT

10

Sca

Based on a co
published b

NEW

Pecos River

TEXAS

MEXICO

AUBRY

AUBRY'S BIRTHPLACE

This photograph shows the house in Maskinongé, Quebec Province, where
François Aubry was born in 1824. The photograph was taken in 1910.

Courtesy, Clément Plante, St. Justin, Quebec

I

Quebec Origins

François-Xavier Aubry dit Francoeur was born in the family home near Maskinongé, Quebec Province, on December 3, 1824, and was baptized the following day in the church in Maskinongé.[1]

There was nothing distinguished about his birth, nor about his family. But in French Canada, where practically everyone is related, the dictates of family history made everyone important. And when one earns international fame, he is subject to even closer scrutiny.

The Aubry family owned a small farm a few miles northwest of Maskinongé, on the little river, Ormière; later the parish of Saint-Justin would be created there. The father, Joseph Aubry, had received the land in 1815 from his father Nicolas. At that time there were no buildings on the land.[2] On June 15, 1818, Joseph Aubry married Magdeleine Lupien in Maskinongé; they were to live at the Saint-Justin farm until 1840 and raise nine children, of whom François-Xavier was the eldest.[3]

---

[1] Parish records in the Archives, Séminaire St-Joseph, Trois-Rivières.

[2] Letter of Dec. 22, 1971, from Clément Plante, St-Justin, Quebec. Mr. Plante has provided information from land records and maps of the region.

[3] Letter from Raymond Gingras, Aug. 8, 1973, Nat. Arch. of Quebec.

The village of Saint-Justin is in the center of the parish of the same name. To the northeast is the River Maskinongé; three smaller rivers also flow through the parish. This is a fertile farming plateau, whose main boundaries are the Saint Lawrence River to the south and mountains to the west. The land was first settled in the late 1600s, the whole being named the Seigneurie de Maskinongé. By the mid-1700s the region which would later become Saint-Justin had a population of about three hundred. The Seigneurie de Carufel was sliced off from that of Maskinongé, and Saint-Justin was created as a separate parish in 1848. One parish history has a subtitle which conveys the spirit of the community: "Home of Rural Serenity." [4]

Because the Aubrys were small farmers with a minimum of interest in things literary and intellectual, there has been some confusion over the Aubry ancestry. In the last century the Canadian historian Benjamin Sulte became fascinated with Aubry's exploits. Among other things, Sulte was interested in the famous Forge of Saint-Maurice, near Trois-Rivières. His research had uncovered a variety of Aubrys who worked at the Forge, including a Nicolas Aubry. Further research, plus interviews with Aubry's brothers, convinced Sulte that the Aubry family had worked at the Forge for several generations.[5] This proved to be erroneous, but several later historians have reported the Forge tradition. The Aubrys had always been small farmers in the New World.

[4] Fr. Hermann Plante, *Saint-Justin: foyer de sérénité rurale,* pp. 9-22.

[5] Benjamin Sulte, "F.-X. Aubry," *Bulletin de Recherches Historiques,* XV (Nov. 1909), 351-52; Sulte, "Les Forges Saint-Maurice," in *Mélanges Historiques,* VI (1920), 87-88, 109.

Of the several Aubry families that came to New France, François-Xavier was in the fourth generation from Nicolas Aubry, who was born in the Diocese of Toul, in Lorraine.[6] Nicolas Aubry was originally a grenadier in the Regiment of Languedoc; he came to the New World with his regiment, and like many of his fellow soldiers he stayed to help settle the land and to protect the settlements against the constant harassment of the Iroquois to the south.[7]

Nicolas married Marie-Anne Juneau in 1759 and farmed near Saint-Augustin, a small village a few miles south of Quebec.[8] The couple most likely moved to the Maskinongé vicinity after a few years, for in 1768 "Nicolas Aubri, dit francoeur" was living in the parish of Carufel, which later became Saint-Justin.[9] Nicolas' son, also named Nicolas, was married there in 1787.[10] It was this Nicolas who first bought the vacant land on the Ormière and gave it to his son Joseph, the father of François-Xavier.

---

[6] Gabriel Drouin, *Dictionnaire National,* I, p. 28.

[7] "La Famille Aubrenan ou Aubry," *Bulletin de Recherches Historiques,* LX (Nov. 1934), 641-44.

[8] Marriage records, Nat. Arch. of Quebec. "Nicolas Aubry dit francoeur de Cyré en Loraine Diocese de Toul" requested bans of marriage to be made public Oct. 20, 1758; records of marriages in *Rapport de l'Archiviste de la Province de Québec, 1951-1953,* p. 22.

[9] List of early settlers in Plante, *Saint-Justin,* pp. 21-22. The name Aubry is supposedly from Albéric, meaning "powerful mountain" in Old German. Spelling variants include Aubri, Aupré, Aupry, Hopris, Auprix, Aubrey, etc.; see *Rapport de l'Archiviste de la Province de Québec, 1951-1953,* p. 526. François-Xavier consistently spelled his name Aubry; most historians have preferred Aubrey.

The *dit Francoeur* is best understood as an additional surname, a common practice among French Canadians. Some were named for places in France *(dit Limousin),* some for birthplaces *(dit Niagara),* others for physical characteristics *(dit Le Grand),* etc.

[10] Marriage records, Nat. Arch. of Quebec.

François-Xavier attended the local school for a few years and learned to read and write, and also became familiar with the basics of arithmetic. Things were not going well for the Aubry family, though. Farming was poor, and became worse. The political revolution in Quebec in 1837-1838 and the severe economic depression of that decade brought extreme poverty to the region. François left school and worked with a Mr. Clément, a local merchant. He then went to nearby Saint-Jean, where he worked in the store of Mr. Marchand.[11]

Joseph Aubry was in such trouble now that in 1840 he was forced to sell his home and land. The Aubry family, minus François, moved to a new homestead region at Saint-Maurice, near Trois-Rivières. But the Aubrys still suffered many hardships.[12]

Early in 1843, François decided to leave Canada. An early biographer recorded an extract from an Aubry letter of May 1 of that year: "It is necessary that I leave, not that I am forced to do so by my misconduct, but to earn more in the hope of helping my parents." [13]

It is not clear what arrangements Aubry made, if any, before he left Quebec for the United States. He arrived in Saint Louis late in 1843 and obtained employment as a clerk with Moise Lamoureux and Elzear Blanchard, French Canadian merchants who had been in Missouri for some years.[14]

---

[11] Joseph Tassé, article on Aubry in *Les Canadiens de l'Ouest,* vol. II, pp. 180-227.

[12] *Ibid.,* p. 180. Clément Plante, letter of Dec. 22, 1971, shows the land sale occurring on Oct. 9, 1840; Mr. Plante also provided a plat map of land along the Ormière River, showing the Aubry family holdings.

[13] Tassé, *Les Canadiens,* II, p. 181.   [14] *Ibid.*

A mid-century trip from Quebec to Saint Louis for a single young man might seem unusual and complicated, but Aubry's later reputation was made as a loner. Furthermore, a French Canadian on the road was never really alone. From the Atlantic to the Pacific there were scattered settlements of French Canadians, and the farther west one went, the more numerous they seemed to be. French Canadians had been in the forefront of exploration, fur trade, and missions, and it was common to see these sons of Quebec in Minnesota, Missouri, New Mexico, Oregon, and California. Aubry had entered a new world, but the adjustment would be smooth because of the presence of his compatriots. Later, in Chihuahua, California, Sonora, Texas, and New Mexico, French pathfinders who had preceded Aubry would help plan exploratory routes with him.

When Aubry arrived in Saint Louis, the Lamoureux and Blanchard store was at 27 South First Street, dealing in dry goods and groceries. Aubry learned English and perfected his written French in his duties as a clerk. He most likely boarded in the Blanchard home at Poplar and Almond Streets.[15]

Soon after Aubry arrived in Saint Louis and began to work, he learned of the death of his father and how the family was now in even more difficult circumstances. Aubry sent his first wages to his mother; from then until his death eleven years later, Aubry would be the main financial support for the numerous family in Quebec.[16]

---

[15] *St. Louis Directory, 1842,* pp. 11, 79.

[16] Tassé, *Les Canadiens,* II, p. 181. Aubry's estate also went to his mother in a long, complicated arrangement ending in the late 1860s; Loose Documents, Archdiocese of Santa Fe, especially 1858 #5, and 1868 #7.

The Quebec origins of Aubry are clear, but in the last century several historians gave a garbled account of his background which was absurd – but was repeated. An 1888 history of Kansas City referred to Aubry as "an enterprising young New York 'Yankee'." As late as 1928 the New York *Times* maintained the "Yankee" Aubry tradition.[17]

---

[17] Theo. S. Case (ed.), *History of Kansas City, Missouri,* p. 35; *New York Times Magazine,* Apr. 1, 1928, p. 21.

❧II❧

To Santa Fe

War with Mexico seemed imminent to most observers in 1846, and in late April of that year the first hostilities between the United States and Mexican forces took place along the Rio Grande. A large segment of the citizens of the United States welcomed a war, especially the residents of the West and South. To them, the territories of Chihuahua, California, New Mexico, and other southern and western lands were logical choices for extension of United States rule.

Twenty-two year old François Aubry was in the midst of a frontier community that could thrive because of such expansion. Saint Louis was a commercial *entrepot* for the West. Bustling docks along the Mississippi, a railroad connection with the East, a river route (the Missouri) to Saint Joseph, and excellent north-south river routes from Minnesota to New Orleans gave the city many advantages.

The entire city, along with many other sections of the country, seemed to be forcing the nation into war. The successful community could become a metropolis if Mexico were to lose her northern provinces. The sphere of influence for Saint Louis could include such distant points as Santa Fe, Monterrey, and Los Angeles. Already Saint Louis was a major receiver and distributor of potatoes, whiskey, sugar, coffee, wheat, hemp, hides, and other products. A successful war, and a major annexation, would work wonders for the Saint Louis trade.[1]

In early May of 1846, General Zachary Taylor's troops defeated an invading Mexican force near the Rio Grande in two major battles. The formal declaration of war came on May 13, and President Polk boldly stated to his cabinet that Mexico would lose the war, and that for indemnity the United States would claim New Mexico, California, and other territory.[2]

A two-pronged attack was planned. An Army of the West was to move towards Santa Fe and then to southern California, where it would link with a naval force to complete the conquest. A second land army was to head south to Mexico City and wrap up what was hoped would be a short war. The Army of the West was headed by Colonel Stephen Watts Kearny, who gathered his force at Fort Leavenworth in late spring. When he set out for Santa Fe on June 30, Kearny commanded three hundred regular dragoons, one thousand Missouri Volunteers, five hundred Mormons, and one thousand "assorted" recruits. One of the tasks of the Army of the West was to protect freight caravans bound from Missouri for New Mexico and Chihuahua.[3]

The traders, in one of the unusual, semi-comic stories of any war, were in advance of the army, and for good

---

[1] A notable increase did indeed occur. In amount and value, most items in St. Louis business doubled from mid-1845 to mid-1846; see "Business of St. Louis," *Daily Missouri Republican,* July 1846.

[2] Ray Allen Billington, *Westward Expansion*, pp. 578-79.

[3] *Ibid.,* p. 579.

SAINT LOUIS IN 1857
The commercial *entrepot* of an expanding West, Saint Louis was booming
in the 1840s when Aubry arrived and began his trading career.
From *Ballou's Pictorial,* Mar. 14, 1857

WESTPORT, MISSOURI
While Aubry was in the Santa Fe Trade, most of the merchants left Missouri
from Westport, which is in the modern Kansas City metropolitan area.
From *Century,* Nov. 1890

AN EVENING ON THE TRAIL
The predominantly male composition of the Santa Fe Trade is exhibited
in this sketch, as opposed to later westward migrations of families.
From *Harper's Weekly,* Dec. 23, 1871

LOADING WAGONS FOR THE TRAIL
From *Harper's Monthly,* July 1880

SAN FRANCISCO STREET
The main street of old Santa Fe, where the excitement
and activity of the town was centered.
From *Harper's Monthly*, April 1880

DANCING AND GAMBLING
Two oft-discussed activities in the town of Santa Fe.
Above, from Beadle, *Undeveloped West,* p. 456;
below, from *Harper's Monthly,* April 1854

reason. The ports of Mexico were to be blockaded, which meant that in the rich inland trading zones of Chihuahua and New Mexico, prices would rise. There were many reasons for the attitude of the traders: confidence in the United States Army, which they knew was on its way; a feeling that the Mexican Army would collapse; and rumors that local rebellions in the northern Mexican states against the central government were already under way.[4]

There was a tinge of respect left for Mexican authority, though. The traders wanted to beat the army to Santa Fe in order to obtain *guias* (custom house permits) from Governor Manuel Armijo, which would allow them to trade in New Mexico and Chihuahua. In spite of impending hostilities, the traders believed that the Mexican Army would not interfere with them if they had permits.[5] Some traders were truly without nationalistic bias; they carried arms and ammunition to sell to the Mexican forces.

Hundreds of traders headed for Santa Fe, caring not at all that war was declared. Word was in also that the Mexican merchants, especially in the northern regions, wanted the trade to continue. So, when Colonel Kearny got underway on June 30, there were hundreds of wagons scattered along the Santa Fe Trail. And it was not

---

[4] Based on Bernard DeVoto, *The Year of Decision:1846,* pp. 228-31. Santa Fe and Chihuahua trade from Missouri was not new, in fact there had been considerable commerce since the 1820s. Even before the outbreak of the war, trade was increasing. For example, in February of 1846 "another company" of traders arrived in Missouri from Chihuahua and New Mexico (7 men and 3 teams), bringing in $35,000; *Daily Missouri Republican,* Feb. 16, 1846. See also *ibid.,* Mar. 26, 1846 ("We learn that this trade will be very considerably increased during the present year.")

[5] George Rutledge Gibson, *Journal of a Soldier under Kearny and Doniphan,* ed. by Ralph Bieber, p. 41.

only merchants who had the urge to go west. Emigrants glutted the streets of Independence, Missouri, in May, purchasing wagons and supplies. They left for Oregon and California in late May, one more complication for Colonel Kearny's troops.[6]

Another menace faced all western travelers, roving bands of Indians who cared not whether the interlopers were United States Army, merchants, Mexican officials, or Mexican farmers. In late April the Apaches and Utes north of Santa Fe had killed several American merchants and run off herds of Mexican cattle. In late May, Comanches attacked several merchant parties approaching Bent's Fort. One of the current rumors was that Governor Armijo in New Mexico had offered the Comanches and Apaches $5 per head for all mules and horses they could steal from Kearny's men.[7]

Young Aubry was stirred by the talk of expansion, increase in trade, money to be made, and adventure. He decided to get in at the beginning by doing what he knew best – business. He obtained credit from Lamoureux and Blanchard, purchased trade goods, and paid the firm of Webb and Doan, Santa Fe traders, $117 for carrying his freight and $15 for board. On May 9, a few days before declaration of war, Aubry set out from Independence, Missouri, with George Doan, James Webb, and other traders for New Mexico. The party arrived in Santa Fe on June 23 without incident.[8]

6 *Daily Missouri Republican,* May 21, 1846; *Niles' National Register,* June 6, 1846, article from Independence dated May 16.

7 *Daily Missouri Republican,* May 11, June 25, Aug. 24, 1846.

8 Tassé, *Les Canadiens,* II, pp. 180-81; Ralph Bieber (ed.), *Exploring Southwestern Trails, 1846-1854,* p. 39; Ross Calvin, "Westward Empire," *New Mex. Mag.,* XXIV (July 1946), 14-15, 41-45.

This was Aubry's first visit to Santa Fe, a city which would become his second home for the next decade. He was in town for a month, but in spite of the presence of the army and the threat of hostilities between Kearny's men and those of Governor Armijo, things were not overly exciting. Business for the arriving traders was seemingly good, but according to Aubry it was "dull." [9]

Foreign visitors to Santa Fe had seldom used the word "dull" when referring to the city. Before the war, the occasional United States visitor or merchant often commented on the city's vices and lack of culture. Richard Wilson and a party of six stayed at Bachelor's Hall in the early 1840s for 25¢ a week and free housekeeping. They lived in grand style next to the Plaza and enjoyed watching the governor visit the nearby billiard parlor for a game; across the street was a large gambling house. The garrison band (3 drummers, 2 fifers, 1 boy on a triangle) marched through the town at noon and at 8:00 P.M., "playing their only song." [10]

Gambling, nightly fandangoes, guitars and violins, an occasional fight — these were part of the foreign stereotype of life in New Mexico. It was, according to many, "a backwash of civilization, isolated, ignorant, and tyrannized." [11] Throw some overly excited Yankee soldiers into this Mexican cultural cauldron and further spicing was sure to take place.

[9] *Daily Missouri Republican,* Aug. 24, 1846; this is Aubry's journal and takes up most of one column.

[10] Richard L. Wilson, *Short Ravelings from a Long Yarn of the Santa Fe Trail,* pp. 148-49.

[11] William Brown, "The Santa Fe Trail," a mimeographed publication of the U.S. Dept. of the Int., National Park Service, 1963; life in Santa Fe, pp. 37-39.

George Ruxton, a British traveler, passed through Santa Fe in late 1846 and called it a "wretched collection of mudhouses . . . the appearance of the town defies description, and I can compare it to nothing but a dilapidated brick-kiln or a prairie-dog town. The inhabitants are worthy of their city, and a more miserable, vicious-looking population it would be impossible to imagine." Every other house was a grocery (whiskey shop), and "everywhere filth and dirt reigned triumphant."

Ruxton, though, cannot be accused of Anglo-Saxon condescension, as he also reported that the town was not improved by the addition of three thousand Americans, "the dirtiest, rowdiest crew I have ever seen collected together." Crowds of drunken Yankee soldiers walked the streets, brawling, gambling, flirting, and in general bringing Yankee culture to the deprived backwoods community.[12]

Aubry ended his stay in Santa Fe on July 16. A traveling party was organized consisting of a Mr. Stephenson, Adam Hill, John McKnight, and two young sons of Dr. Henry Connelly of Chihuahua. Trader McKnight had arrived in Santa Fe from Chihuahua in early July. The group traveled in two wagons and followed the Cimarron route, reaching Independence without incident on August 17. In Independence the group split up; Aubry and McKnight boarded the river steamer *Balloon* and arrived in Saint Louis on August 22. Aubry had kept a journal during the trip,

12 George Frederick Ruxton, *Wild Life in the Rocky Mountains*, ed. by Horace Kephart, pp. 61-62.

and he showed it to the editor of the *Daily Missouri Republican,* who thanked Aubry for the journal, "which we were kindly permitted to copy." [13]

So Aubry's reporting career had begun. During the next eight years his journals and letters would appear throughout the nation's press, especially in those areas where new settlements and transportation questions were of interest. Soon "Frank" Aubry was a close friend of editors in Saint Louis, Santa Fe, and Independence. His journals were admired because they were thorough, yet clear, and only mildly optimistic. Difficulties were not hidden; Indian attacks, food and water problems, and climate were accurately reported.

His first printed journal is representative of the dozens that followed. He surveyed the opinion in Santa Fe regarding the new Yankee take-over and suggested (accurately) that General Kearny would meet little or no resistance there. He also recorded the costs per pound and per wagon for freighting on the Santa Fe Trail. The duty (sum paid to Mexican authorities in Santa Fe) had averaged $625 per wagon load for merchants who had left from Missouri in the spring.

From the time he left Santa Fe, Aubry recorded every party of traders and soldiers met along the way, such as "On the 3d of August, met twelve government wagons at Coon creek;" "8th, met Magoffin's party at Turkey creek." On August 10, Aubry met twenty-one government wagons at Diamond Spring, and thirty more the next day at Council Grove. On August 13 he

---

[13] Journal appeared in issue of Aug. 24, 1846. For details of the return trip, see Louise Barry, *The Beginning of the West: Annals of the Kansas Gateway to the American West, 1540-1854,* p. 638.

met the Company of Missouri Volunteers from Platte and Monroe counties.

Grass and water were plentiful on the trail, but Aubry doubted that Kearny's command in New Mexico could obtain satisfactory supplies there. This was good news for Aubry and other traders, as they would be called on to supply the army in Santa Fe from Missouri.[14]

The result of the Missouri-Santa Fe-Missouri trip was a neat profit: $100,000. Contrary to some reports, this was not Aubry's share but was the entire amount returned with the group. Some of the party stayed in Independence, and McKnight and Aubry arrived in Saint Louis with "between 50 and 60,000 dollars in specie." Aubry's expenses were minor – a few hundred dollars – so he most likely made several thousand dollars on his first independent venture after repaying Lamoureux and Blanchard.[15]

For the next half-year in Aubry's life there is very little information. In October he visited the Upper Mississippi River towns of Galena, Saint Pierre, and Prairie-du-Chien, on the lookout for a good business investment. He also met and talked with many French Canadians along the way. According to one source, Aubry was even in business "in one place" for a few months and did quite well. But in late winter or early spring of 1847 he was back in Saint Louis, making plans to enter the Santa Fe trade in earnest.[16] Restlessness and

---

14 *Daily Missouri Republican,* Aug. 24, 1846.

15 Correct figures are in *ibid.* and in Barry, *Beginning of the West,* p. 638. An example of imagination is Calvin, *New Mex. Mag.,* XXIV (July 1946), 14-15: "He was back safe in Missouri with the proceeds of his venture – $100,000 in silver coin!"   16 Tassé, *Les Canadiens,* II, p. 181.

the wish to see new country would always be dominant in the Aubry character. It is impossible to imagine his being content to run a small store on the Upper Mississippi, which was already losing its frontier nature.

The Santa Fe trade appealed to Aubry for many reasons. Not only was it a new environment almost a thousand miles away, but there was challenge – and a chance for profit. As the newspapers had reported, "provender of every description is exceedingly scarce," and the Santa Fe grazing lands had not had a rain in more than three months.[17] Opportunity and excitement were on the trail and in Santa Fe, not clerking in Saint Louis or selling bolts of cloth to the farmers around Prairie-du-Chien.

---

[17] *Daily Missouri Republican,* Aug. 20, 1846.

·III·

Big Business

In the spring of 1847, Aubry approached his former employers, Lamoureux and Blanchard, and a few other merchants. Although he was still a young man, he had no trouble raising $6,000 so he could purchase wagons and supplies for the Santa Fe trade.[1]

On April 17, 1847, the following notice appeared in the *Daily Missouri Republican:*

> LETTERS FOR SANTA FE – Mr. F. X. Aubry will leave on Tuesday next for Santa Fe. Letters and papers will be taken charge of by Mr. A. if left at the Republican office.

At this time the only postal service to New Mexico was an infrequent army express from Fort Leavenworth. A considerable number of people had business or personal letters to send, so they took advantage of Aubry's offer. This was his first "courier" job.[2]

Aubry picked up the mail at the Republican office on April 20 and headed for the Town of Kansas (now

---

[1] Tassé, *Les Canadiens,* II, p. 182. Some nonsense was written by D. M. Grissom in 1899 that Aubry got his start in the 1830s as a clerk in the carpet store of Eugene Kelly, later a prominent New York banker; *Encyclopedia of the History of St. Louis,* I, p. 60. This absurd tale was further twisted over the years, as Aubry was converted into a New York merchant.

[2] Bieber, *Exploring Southwestern Trails,* p. 40.

Kansas City). On April 27 the Aubry caravan set out from there and Aubry, with the mail, left Missouri on April 30. He joined the caravan after a few days. Independence and Westport were the leading centers for merchants going to Santa Fe at this time. By the early 1850s steamers could go as far as Westport Landing, so this gradually replaced Independence as the jump-off point. Kansas City developed as a "suburb" of Westport.[3]

This, Aubry's first independent trip, was marked by several disturbing incidents. Before they reached Fort Mann, one of Aubry's men was killed. He had been walking ahead of the caravan when an Indian shot him with an arrow from ambush, ran up and scalped him, and escaped before startled onlookers could react. This happened within gunshot range of the wagon train.[4]

On June 24 the Aubry train reached Fort Mann in western Kansas. This was a crude stockade that had been erected by Missouri Volunteers below the Cimarron Crossing of the Arkansas. When Aubry reached the fort it had been "militarily" abandoned, but two men were in the stockade, firing at a band of Indians who had kept them surrounded for two days. The men had been trying to overtake another caravan when they were spotted by the Indians. Aubry and his men dispersed the Indians, released the two men, and welcomed them to the caravan.[5]

For the rest of the journey Aubry warned all trav-

[3] Walker D. Wyman, "Freighting: A Big Business on the Santa Fe Trail," *Kansas Hist. Quar.*, I (1931-32), 17-27.

[4] James Josiah Webb, *Adventures in the Santa Fe Trade, 1844-1847*, ed. by Ralph Bieber, pp. 287-88.

[5] *Ibid.;* see also Barry, *Beginning of the West*, p. 675.

elers going east about the Indian menace. A few days
after the Fort Mann incident he met James J. Webb.
Aubry told Webb that the Indians could easily have
taken the two men at the fort, but not without losing a
few warriors. In Webb's words, "there was not sufficient booty (aside from the scalps) to justify the risk." [6]

A caravan on the trail at this time was a conglom-
eration of men and wagons, often with little in common,
even among themselves. In the pre-war days a variety
of farm wagons, road wagons, and "dearborns" were
used, drawn by oxen or mules, carrying a variety of
weights and an even greater variety of goods.

In 1839 Governor Manuel Armijo of New Mexico
imposed an import fee of $500 per wagon. The Amer-
ican traders then had to plan for larger wagons to make
the trip worthwhile. By the time of the Mexican War
most of the vehicles on the trail were Pittsburgh wagons, built in Pittsburgh and shipped to Missouri by
steamer.[7]

Usually eight oxen, or like number of mules, drew
each wagon, although if ten or twelve mules were used,
about five thousand pounds of cargo could be carried.
Oxen were strong, but mules were better for a variety
of reasons. Josiah Gregg claimed that the inferiority of
oxen was "partially owing to the tenderness of their
feet." [8]

Oxen were superior for pulling through sandy or
muddy trails, but they did not fare so well as mules on
the short, dry prairie grass. Mules cost more than oxen,

[6] Webb, *Adventures in the Santa Fe Trade,* pp. 287-88.

[7] Henry Pickering Walker, *The Wagonmasters,* pp. 96-97.

[8] Josiah Gregg, *The Commerce of the Prairies,* ed. by Milo M. Quaife, pp.
22-24.

but they lasted longer and traveled faster. Aubry, with his interest in speed, naturally preferred mules to oxen.[9]

Saint Louis and other Missouri cities and towns were beginning to manufacture wagons, but it was only in the late 1840s that local production could meet the demand. Many traders were not happy with the Pittsburgh wagons. In one instance some traders arrived at Fort Bent grumbling about the time spent in repairing the wagons, and "the timber in them was not that with which they started."[10]

Joseph Murphy of Saint Louis developed what was to become the typical freight wagon of the Santa Fe Trail. By the late 1840s his wagons were rivalling the "Pittsburghs." The huge vehicle had a bed sixteen feet long, was six feet high, and had rear wheels seven feet in diameter. Murphy used seasoned woods and developed a method of boring holes with hot iron rather than an auger; this prevented rotting or cracking around the bolts.[11]

Food for the trip for each man consisted of fifty pounds of flour, fifty pounds of bacon, ten pounds of coffee, twenty pounds of sugar, and a little salt. Gregg claimed that beans and crackers were luxuries seldom found on the trail. But the main item on the menu was good: buffalo, "and great is the joy of the traveler when that noble animal first appears in sight." Frying pan, kettle, coffee pot, tin cup, and a butcher's knife were on hand, and the men sat down on the grass, joked, and

9 *Ibid.,* pp. 23-24.
10 Pittsburgh wagon controversy in *Daily Missouri Republican,* Sept. 9 & 30, 1846.   11 Walker, *Wagonmasters,* pp. 96-97.

"from their greasy hands they swallow their savory viands."[12]

Clothing was a frontier grab-bag: leather hunting shirts, blue jean coats, flannel sleeve vests, and the "fustian frock of the city-bred merchant." All of the men carried firearms, rifles for hunting, and scatter-guns for birds or for defense during night attacks. The men also had a variety of pistols and knives.[13]

The phrase "Santa Fe trade" is handy, but misleading. By the late 1830s half of the goods shipped to Santa Fe were then taken to El Paso, Chihuahua, and other points south. As Saint Louis was the gathering point for men and goods, so was Santa Fe the receiver and distributor. Often, Santa Fe was merely a stop along the way for traders bound for Chihuahua. Because the trade was over the Santa Fe Trail, many have assumed the city, not the region, was the final destination.[14]

The city of Chihuahua was more than five hundred miles south of Santa Fe, on the road to Mexico City. Chihuahua was twice as large as Santa Fe. Before the Mexican War, Chihuahua merchants considered Santa Fe – and all of New Mexico – a dumping ground for all second-rate goods. Once the war started, though, the Mexican ports were blockaded, and Chihuahua was cut off from her imports. As a result, many merchants from Missouri who got as far as Santa Fe decided to go further south to Chihuahua, a larger potential market.[15]

By the time of the Mexican War the trade on the trail

[12] Gregg, *Commerce of the Prairies*, pp. 22, 43-44.
[13] *Ibid.*, pp. 36-37.   [14] Brown, "Santa Fe Trail," p. 39.
[15] Walker, *Wagonmasters*, pp. 131-32.

had risen to half a million pounds of merchandise a
year. It rose rapidly during the period when Aubry
became a trader (late 1840s). The United States Army
had to be fed and clothed, and the entire Southwest had
a new population which had to be supplied.

A brief notice in the *Daily Missouri Republican* in
July of 1846 announced that the steamer *Tom Corwin*
had just docked in Saint Louis with "Santa Fe goods,"
1,373 packages, or 150 tons.[16] This was to be a common
occurrence, later not even worth a newspaper comment.

What was carried in the hundreds of wagons bound
for Santa Fe and points beyond? Almost anything that
could be found in small stores scattered throughout the
United States. Cotton goods were leading commodities,
but Mexico needed almost all types of manufactured
goods: clothing, rings, necklaces, mirrors, writing
paper, liquor of all kinds – the list is long. Gregg also
mentions pocket-knives, hats, cutlery, and calicoes.[17] All
types of clothing were in demand. The New York
Clothing Emporium of Saint Louis announced in the
summer of 1847 that Santa Fe traders could stop in to
select from the five hundred Mackinaw blanket coats,
just in by steamer.[18]

Other leading commodities were groceries, leather,
hosiery, and grain. Although traders differed, as did
the year and the demand, the bulk of the freight during the 1846-1850 era consisted of flour, ammunition,
whiskey, and hardware.[19]

---

16 Issue of July 17, 1846.

17 Brown, "Santa Fe Trail," pp. 39-40; Gregg, *Commerce of the Prairies,*
pp. 279-80.   18 *Daily Missouri Republican,* Aug. 19, 1847 (adv.).

19 Wyman, *Kansas Hist. Quar.,* I (1931-32), 17-27.

The invoices and other business records of James J. Webb, Santa Fe merchant, have survived. Some of the goods he handled during this era included hair oil, face powder, crockery, India ink, wax, matches, feathers, nails, gun locks, pen holders, playing cards, Spanish dictionaries, figs, sardines, files, hand saws, iodine, canned peaches and pears, shaving brushes, razors, cigars, and so forth, almost anything the Mexicans, or new settlers, needed.[20]

Hundreds of men, many of them leading merchants, were concerned with pushing the commerce to Santa Fe and Chihuahua. Many became wealthy and powerful on the frontier: Josiah Gregg, William McKnight, Alexander Majors, Ceran St. Vrain, George Doan, James Webb are a few. In this company Aubry did not merely wish to succeed, he intended to excel.

The Aubry caravan reached Santa Fe in early July. He disposed of his goods within a week and arranged for a departure before the end of the month. In the few weeks he was in Santa Fe, Aubry seems to have seen and spoken to everyone of consequence: travelers, soldiers, merchants, and even some Chihuahua businessmen. He would later transmit all of what he learned to an eager newspaper public in Missouri.[21]

On July 28, Aubry left Santa Fe for Missouri with a Mr. Barnum, just in from Chihuahua, Captain McKinney's company of volunteers from Monroe County, Missouri, and a train of sixty-five government wagons. Because of the size of the party there were no Indian

[20] Ralph Paul Bieber, "The Papers of James J. Webb, Santa Fe Merchant, 1846-1861," *Wash. Univ. Studies,* Vol. XI, Humanistic Ser. (Apr. 1924), 299-301.   [21] *Daily Missouri Republican,* Sept. 6, 1847.

problems. Somewhere near Pawnee Fork, Aubry left the party and raced on alone for his first attempt at speed. He reached Independence on August 31, making three hundred miles in the last four days, an unprecedented time. An additional incentive for speed was the large sack of mail with which he had been entrusted. On September 6, Aubry arrived in Saint Louis by steamer.[22]

According to one source, Aubry swung a shrewd business deal while on the trail. He sold his wagons and mules to another eastbound group for $6,000, which covered all his debts. The sales in Santa Fe, then, represented pure profit.[23]

In this era of chaos and uncertainty in the new Southwest, accurate news was in demand. The correspondent of the *Daily Missouri Republican* interviewed Aubry for "news that will be interesting" as soon as Aubry arrived in Independence. The major item was the murder in Chihuahua, of James Aull whose store was robbed of $5,000. Aull was from a prominent Missouri merchant family. Even though the murderers were immediately arrested and jailed, Missouri merchants feared the death of Aull would handicap further Chihuahua trade. Even Governor Armijo of New Mexico, traveling in Chihuahua, was arrested because he displayed sympathy for recent United States military victories. Aubry also filled in with news of the territorial elections in New Mexico, troop movements in the region, and general attitudes of Mexican nationals towards Missouri merchants.[24]

---

[22] Barry, *Beginning of the West,* 713-14; *Daily Missouri Republican,* Sept. 7, 1847.   [23] Tassé, *Les Canadiens,* II, p. 182.
[24] *Daily Missouri Republican,* Sept. 6, 1847.

Aubry, again, had kept a journal of his return trip; the *Republican* printed most of the August entries. Here was news of American merchant, Indian, and military life along a route of eight hundred miles. Aubry threw in dozens of names of soldiers, merchants, and other travelers. William McKnight and twenty wagons were met at Middle Spring on August 12; on August 29, at Council Grove, he met St. Vrain's twenty wagons. Aubry even listed the names of "middle" personnel, such as "Mr. Hays, Indian trader," "Messrs. White & Simpson, Sutlers to Rall's Regiment," "Coffman, of Platte, wagon master." Events of interest were also recorded: "W. B. Howell of Simonds company, died a little below the Middle Spring." [25]

One daily entry will suffice to show the variety and type of information Aubry provided: "August 10th – Met, at Cold Spring, a company of mounted Missouri volunteers, under charge of Capt. Jones, who had two pieces of artillery along. Emanuel Armijo is in company, with nine wagons."

Aubry's journal ran in the issue of September 6 (sent in from Independence), and he arrived in Saint Louis on the same day. The *Republican* editor pumped him for additional news, especially about new troop assignments in New Mexico. [26] The editor also related important mail news. Aubry had brought in key letters and dispatches, and "a large mail in the wagon behind, would arrive in a few days."

The impression here is of a city anxious to get any news of its native sons scattered on the frontier, especially of the dozens of volunteer companies serving in

[25] *Ibid.*   [26] *Ibid.*, Sept. 7, 1847.

the war. Others besides Aubry would provide information, but his many details and reliable opinions made a greater impact on the newspaper people. And, more important, Aubry's news was always the "fastest."

September was the end of the normal trading season – but not for Aubry. He immediately bought merchandise and supplies for a second trip in a single season. A notice appeared in the *Republican* of September 9:

> FOR SANTA FE – Mr. Aubry, who returned from Santa Fe two or three days since, will leave for the same destination on Friday evening next. He will take charge of any letters for persons in that quarter, if left at this office by 12 o'clock on Friday.

This meant, then, that Aubry would be in Saint Louis only four days before leaving for western Missouri to make final arrangements for the journey.

This time Aubry headed for Independence instead of Westport. At Independence Aubry joined with A. P. Boggs and Alonzo Kean; they finished hiring hands and buying wagons and left for Santa Fe on September 25. Their merchandise consisted of fifteen wagons loaded with easily-salable items, worth about $40,000. As usual, it was not Aubry's intention to remain long in one place.[27]

Most of the trip was uneventful, but as they neared Santa Fe they had some excitement. Aubry and three of his men decided to arrive in town in advance of the wagons. They left the caravan at the Red River crossing, but a few miles later they were surprised and chased fifteen miles towards a town on the River Moro by approximately fifty Indians who were on foot. One

---

27 *El Republicano,* Oct. 30, 1847; Tassé, *Les Canadiens,* II, p. 182; Barry, *Beginning of the West,* p. 719.

of the mules gave out, and they barely made it to town; the Indians followed to the outskirts.[28]

This was one of the times Aubry regretted not having horses. He had no use for oxen, loved mules for pulling wagons and for regular trail riding, but preferred horses when speed was required.

Aubry and his three companions arrived in Santa Fe on October 29, and the wagons arrived the following day. This gave him a remarkable mercantile advantage; he had made two trips in one trading "season." While other merchants stayed in Missouri, fearing the winter cold and snows, Aubry was in Santa Fe peddling much-needed goods. Aubry gave the editor what news he had of Saint Louis and the trail, and he also carried two issues of the *Daily Missouri Republican,* which the Santa Fe editor extracted for his columns.[29]

There were many changes in Santa Fe since the United States takeover the year before. Several hotels and private boarding houses were operating – even putting on doors, windows, "and other marks of improvement." New buildings were being erected, and business in general was good.[30]

On November 13 the following advertisement appeared in the *Santa Fe Republican:* "Gin, Brandy and Port Wine, for sale by F. X. AUBREY." In the Spanish section of the same issue Aubry announced that he also had groceries, sugar, and beans.[31] Others were in for some of the cash flow in the booming town; in the same

---

[28] News from New Mexico in *Daily Missouri Republican,* Dec. 20, 1847.

[29] *El Republicano,* Oct. 30, 1847.

[30] *Daily Missouri Republican,* Nov. 9, 1847.

[31] *El Republicano* and *Santa Fe Republican* were names for the same newspaper; throughout its brief career the paper usually carried Spanish as well as English columns.

issue was an announcement of a new establishment offering hardware, clothing, and food, operated by St. Vrain and Bent, owners of Bent's Fort on the Arkansas.

Within two weeks Aubry had sold all his merchandise. He had no permanent store in town and most likely sold from his wagons parked on the Plaza. It is possible, though, that he used the store of his friends, Joseph and Henri Mercure, fellow French Canadians located on the Plaza.

The local newspaper reported that Aubry planned to return to Missouri about December 25, and that he would be happy to deliver any letters and papers.[32] On December 11 the *Republican* notified its readers that Aubry would make "one of his expeditious trips" between December 20 and 25: "We may recommend him to all who have business in the U.S. as an attentive and active gentleman who will do all he proposes." Aubry left Santa Fe on the morning of December 22, intending to make the trip in eighteen days, "which we have no doubt he will accomplish, as he is one of nature's most persevering children." [33]

Although Aubry had speed in mind for the return trip to Missouri, he was handicapped by others in his traveling party. When the group left Santa Fe on December 22, Aubry was accompanied by four of his men and one servant, a free Negro named Pompey. The men gradually tired, and dropped back; even Aubry's servant gave up sixty miles west of Council Grove.[34]

Aubry dashed the last three days, averaging one hundred miles a day, and reached Independence on Jan-

32 *El Republicano*, Nov. 27, 1847.   33 *Ibid.*, Dec. 25, 1847.
34 *Daily Missouri Republican*, Jan. 11 & 18, 1848; Bieber, *Exploring Southwestern Trails*, 42.

uary 5, 1848, fourteen days from Santa Fe. Along the way he had been attacked and robbed of ten mules by Mexican bandits, had four days of severe cold weather, was delayed half a day by Indians, lost half a day in a snow storm, and killed three mules by hard riding.[35]

On January 4, a day from the end of his dash, Aubry met Jim Beckwourth on the trail, and they exchanged little more than greetings, as they were both in a hurry. Aubry was carrying a "mail," and Beckwourth was carrying dispatches from Fort Leavenworth to Santa Fe.[36]

With such meteoric trail riding, Aubry had little chance to talk with westbound travelers, nor to keep a journal. As usual, though, when he reached Missouri he was interviewed by newspaper men – not only for news, but for details of his dash across the plains. The situation in Santa Fe was fairly calm, so aside from a few comments on the town and mention of the deplorable state of affairs at Fort Mann (lack of supplies, no discipline, etc.), there was little to report.[37] Aubry also talked with merchant Robert Aull upon his return; according to Aubry the situation in Chihuahua was deteriorating. Communications with the States were prohibited by the Mexican government, and Aubry believed that the traders' goods would soon be confiscated. This was a further blow to Aull, whose brother had been killed earlier in the year in Chihuahua.[38]

---

[35] Good summaries of the ride are in Bieber, *Exploring Southwestern Trails*, 41-42, and Barry, *Beginning of the West*, 730-31. The best contemporary accounts are in *Daily Missouri Republican*, Jan. 11 & 18, 1848.

[36] *Santa Fe Republican*, Feb. 12, 1848.

[37] *Daily Missouri Republican*, Jan. 18, 1848.

[38] Letter of Robert Aull to Thomas Larkin, Jan. 15, 1848, in *Missouri Hist. Soc. Coll.*, v (1927-28), 302. Aull ran a store in Lexington, Mo., where he kept in touch with his family and other partners in the trail trade.

The speed of the Aubry trip was such that it broke the previous record by ten and a half days, set by Norris Colburn in August 1846.[39] Aubry stayed about a week in Independence and arrived in Saint Louis on January 17, where he was again sought out by journalists.[40] The residents of Saint Louis knew what trail riding was, so the praise for Aubry had some meaning. The *Republican* made an unequivocal judgement of the trip: "Such a rate of travel is unprecedented in Prairie life, and speaks much in favor of Mr. A.'s indisputable courage and perseverance."[41]

The challenges of the trail, the opening of a new territory, were subjects that interested others besides the populace of Missouri. Aubry was now a national figure, known for his speed and for his reporting. On January 29, 1848, on page one, the *New York Weekly Tribune* acknowledged that its comments on the proceedings of the Mexican legislature came from Aubry, telegraphed in from the paper's correspondent in Independence. The *Tribune* also wrote: "Mr. Aubrey is just in from the prairies, having performed the trip from Santa Fe . . . in fourteen days. The last three days of his trip he averaged upward of one hundred miles a day."

The Indian activity had been perilous; on three of the four trail legs, Aubry had been attacked. Other traders also received attention. Throughout the 1847 season, 47 Americans had been killed, 330 wagons destroyed, and 6,500 animals stolen. Near Fort Mann the Pawnees, Comanches, and Kiowas were responsible, but

---

[39] Bieber, *Exploring Southwestern Trails*, p. 42. Colburn made the trip in twenty-four and a half days.

[40] *Daily Missouri Republican*, Jan. 18, 1848.   [41] *Ibid.*, Jan. 11, 1848.

near the Canadian and into Santa Fe the Jicarilla Apaches and Utes were dominant.[42] Aubry was more vulnerable than other traders. He needed speed, so he seldom linked up with other trains, and often he left his caravan and proceeded ahead, either alone or with a small party.

---

[42] Report of Lt. Col. W. Gilpin from Ft. Mann, Aug. 1, 1848, pp. 136-40 in U.S., House, Exec. Doc. #1, *Annual Report, Secy. of War,* 30th Cong., 2nd sess. (1848-49). Gilpin included figures for all of 1847 and the first part of 1848.

❧IV❧

Money and Fame

I without hesitation rank Aubry as the supreme rider in the great riding tradition of the West.   J. Frank Dobie [1]

Dobie's evaluation was not unique. Aubry's contemporaries, and a few historians, have placed him above all riders. Yet one searches in vain for a sketch of him in the nation's biographical publications. The greatest rider of all time merits not even a footnote. And the man who made as many as three trips to Santa Fe in a single season, where other traders were content with one, is ignored in most business histories of the trail. [2]

Aubry made three trading trips to Santa Fe in 1848 and became rich. This was an important year for him as he combined business with fame. The trading expeditions were larger now, as he was in a position to buy more wagons, and other merchants and travelers sought the company of this daring and successful frontiersman.

For his first trip he left Independence on March 16,

---

[1] Dobie's article "Saga of the Saddle," *Southwest Review,* XIII (Jan. 1928), 127-47.

[2] For example, Walker's *Wagonmasters,* a well-documented study, does not mention Aubry. Another oft-cited work is R. L. Duffus, *The Santa Fe Trail,* but he mentions Aubry only twice, neither time as the leading merchant he was.

weeks in advance of other traders, with fifteen wagons.[3]
He was also carrying another mail, including important
business papers for Robert Aull. He took enough corn
with him to last until Fort Mann; from that point on
prairie grass would be adequate for his animals. This
early start caused extra expenses, as wagons and some
supplies were hard to obtain. Yet he had the opportunity to reach Santa Fe before the other traders, and
could expect a large profit.[4]

Aubry had tried to take care of Indian problems
along the trail by packing his own artillery. In February he had written to the Secretary of War, asking to
borrow a six-pounder cannon from the Saint Louis
Arsenal. However, Aubry left for New Mexico before
he could learn that this unusual request had been turned
down, private armies being a subject the government
did not even know how to discuss.[5]

Aubry reached Santa Fe on April 21, and his wagons
arrived a few days later, while other traders were still
in Missouri. On May 3, Aubry placed an advertisement
in the *Santa Fe Republican* as a dealer in dry goods,
groceries, boots, shoes, and hardware; it was his intention to sell out in a few weeks and head back for Missouri. The *Republican* praised the young trader, wrote
that no one was more deserving of success, and claimed
that "his word is as good as the State Bank of Missouri." [6]

The newspaper carried excerpts from Missouri

[3] Summaries of the departure are in Bieber, *Exploring Southwestern Trails*,
pp. 43-44, and Barry, *Beginning of the West*, p. 740.

[4] Robert Aull to Samuel H. Woodson, Mar. 9, 1848, *Missouri Hist. Soc. Coll.*,
v (1927-28), 304; St. Louis *Daily Reveille*, Mar. 19, 1848.

[5] Summarized from Bieber, *Exploring Southwestern Trails*, p. 43.

[6] Advertisement and article on Aubry in *Santa Fe Republican*, May 3, 1848.

papers about Aubry's business sense and reliability. He had a "praiseworthy public spirit" and "overcame every obstacle." What amazed the editors was that Aubry had recently become a stock-holder in the Independence and Missouri River Railroad, even though he had no real estate holdings. Unselfishness was thus another attribute assigned to Aubry.[7]

The newspaper advertising, the praise, and the fact that he was the first trader of the season in Santa Fe gave Aubry a tremendous business advantage. He sold out his stock of goods at wholesale before his wagons came into town.[8]

Aubry rested in Santa Fe for a few weeks, then announced that he would leave for Missouri soon and would make the trip within ten days. "If energy and perseverance can accomplish a feat of that kind, Aubry is the man," wrote the *Republican*.[9]

On the evening of May 19 Aubry and six others left Santa Fe and headed east.[10] As usual, others could not keep up with the Aubry pace. After going about three hundred miles, the six fell back, and once again Aubry was a lone prairie rider, having for company a few horses and mules.

The trip was a near disaster, as he killed three horses and two mules by hard riding, was three days without food, was captured and robbed of provisions and the mail by Comanches (he escaped at night), slept only a few hours in almost a week, and walked forty miles to Fort Mann, where he bought a fresh mount. During the trip he lost most of his baggage, provisions, papers, and

[7] *Ibid.;* articles excerpted from Independence *Western Expositor.*
[8] Bieber, *Exploring Southwestern Trails,* p. 44.
[9] *Santa Fe Republican,* May 15, 1848.   [10] *Ibid.,* May 21, 1848.

some letters that he was delivering to the States. He arrived in Independence an hour before sunrise on the morning of May 28, the time of the trip being eight days and ten hours. The *Daily Missouri Republican* phrase, "such traveling is unexampled," was echoed by the nation's press.[11]

The speed of the trip was such that the editor of the *Republican* pointed out that Aubry left Santa Fe twenty-six days *after* the mail, yet arrived at Independence ahead of it.[12]

Several Saint Louis newspapers printed accounts of the trip, based on an extra published by the Independence *Expositor*. Aubry mentioned that Colonel William Gilpin's Missouri Volunteers were on the trail trying to track down Comanches, and this supposedly so infuriated the Indians that they increased the number of attacks on passing caravans and other travelers.[13]

Aubry quickly bought enough merchandise in Saint Louis for thirty wagons and had it shipped to western Missouri, where his next expedition was to be organized. By mid-July Aubry's thirty wagons were on the trail. He may have left with another party, because at the Arkansas Crossing in late July there were about sixty wagons in the train, "for the most part owned by Aubrey." [14]

---

[11] Contemporary accounts in *St. Louis Daily Union*, June 5, 1848; *Daily Missouri Republican*, June 3, 1848; *Daily Reveille*, June 3, 1848; *New York Herald*, June 13, 1848; *New York Weekly Tribune*, June 17, 1848; *Santa Fe Republican*, June 9, 1848; see also Barry, *Beginning of the West*, pp. 753-54.

[12] *Daily Missouri Republican*, June 3, 1848.

[13] This is based on *Daily Reveille*, June 3, 1848; I have not been able to locate a copy of the *Expositor* extra.

[14] Barry, *Beginning of the West*, p. 764. He most likely left from Independence.

This stop provided a chance encounter which led to a good description of Aubry and trail life. Lieutenant George D. Brewerton, United States Army, was also camped there. At first Brewerton had no interest in the new arrivals, as a new group was met almost daily. Then, when informed that Aubry was there, Brewerton regained interest. "As 'Little Aubrey' had become as familiar an appellation among Western men as a Jake Hawkins rifle, I determined to go over and pay my respects forthwith."

At the corral he found Aubry and a few friends seated on the ground, where a gaudy blanket had been set as a table. Introductions were made, and Aubry invited Brewerton to "take prairie fare, if I could eat fat cow."

After making his toilet in prairie fashion, "by giving yourself a succession of shakes," Brewerton joined the Aubry crew. With tin cup and pewter plate they all dipped into the three-legged iron pot. Conclusion: "Buffalo meat ain't bad, 'specially fat cow."

After eating, the men smoked fine cigars, talked, and had brandy and water, "for few men are teetolalers if they can help it when west of Council Grove." According to Brewerton, Aubry was a slender man of medium height with keen eyes, iron nerve, great resolution, and indomitable perseverance. The lieutenant was especially impressed with Aubry's lightning-like rides.

The assessment by Brewerton was not a quick look by an Easterner who had merely touched the fringe of the frontier. Brewerton had just returned from an adventure-filled journey across the country from Los Angeles with Kit Carson; in fact, Brewerton believed that

Aubry and Carson were very similar, both in courage and in physical appearance. Years later the Brewerton encounter with Aubry appeared in *Harper's Monthly*.[15]

Aubry, or "The Telegraph," or "Skimmer of the Plains," as he was often called, reached Santa Fe on August 5, again in advance of his wagons. After commenting on Aubry's speed, the Santa Fe newspaper added: "The enterprise that is capable of accomplishing such Herculean tasks, certainly deserves, and we sincerely hope, will receive the most ample reward." For news of immediate interest Aubry told of Colonel Gilpin's continued efforts to make the trail safe, as he fought engagements with the Pawnees on the Cimarron and with the Comanches near Fort Mann. Aubry also reported the new change of government in France, but one wonders how many citizens of Santa Fe were anxious for that news.[16]

Aubry placed advertisements in English and Spanish, announcing that his goods would arrive in a few days and would be for sale, wholesale for cash: dry goods, shoes, boots, groceries, and hardware.[17] Again, Aubry was sold out before his wagons arrived. Because of his preference for wholesaling, he had no need of a building, and sold out of his wagons parked on the Plaza.

The day after he arrived Aubry was drawn into a meeting in the court house of merchants who were protesting the import duty imposed on goods coming into Santa Fe. New Mexico was now a part of the United

---

15 George D. Brewerton, "In the Buffalo Country," *Harper's New Monthly Mag.*, XXV (Aug. 1862), 447-66.

16 "Mr. F. X. Aubry – This gentleman travels with a rapidity almost supernatural;" *Santa Fe Republican*, Aug. 9, 1848.

17 *Ibid.; El Republicano*, Aug. 15, 1848.

States, and the merchants felt that such duties were unconstitutional. Aubry and Manuel Alvarez, William McKnight, Wade Hampton, and a dozen or so other prominent merchants signed a petition urging the territorial government to prohibit such duties.[18]

At this time Aubry was too geared up for travel to linger in Santa Fe. He wanted to get back to Missouri in time for an impossible third trip of the season. He also, of course, wished to gain further fame by breaking his own speed record. On September 12 the *Republican* announced that Aubry would leave in a few hours:

> We wish him a safe journey and a safe return, as we should be happy to see N. Mexico settled by just such enterprising young men. Mr. A. has the credit of making the quickest trip to the States as yet, and we believe that it is his intention to travel at his utmost speed, as his business prompts his immediate service.

In later years there was much talk of bets placed by Aubry on these trips. The figures go from $1,000 to $10,000, but the hard evidence is thin. However, Aubry did tell Brewerton that for his previous ride he wagered a large sum that he would "come in within his time." In New Mexico, "money up" seldom went begging, and soon there were many "tens" and "twenties" against Aubry.[19] It is most likely, then, that Aubry also encouraged bets for his September dash.

Aubry left Santa Fe at dawn of September 12 with a few extra saddled horses. He was astride his favorite yellow mare, Dolly. He had stationed a few horses along the trail, and also believed that he could buy

---

[18] *Santa Fe Republican,* Aug. 16, 1848, contains summaries of meetings held on August 6 and 8.

[19] Brewerton, *Harper's New Monthly Magazine,* xxv (Aug. 1862), 447-66.

fresh mounts from other travelers as needed. His object: make the Santa Fe-Independence trip within six days.

One solid account by an eye-witness to the trip remains, that of merchant Alexander Majors of western Missouri, who was traveling to Santa Fe with a party of twenty-five wagons. About one hundred miles out of Santa Fe, Majors saw a man approaching at a gallop, mounted on a yellow mare and leading another. As the rider came nearer he hesitated, whirled and retreated for fifty yards, until he saw the wagons come around a hill. Satisfied of no Indian trouble, Aubry put spurs to his horse and dashed past, "merely nodding his head as the dust flew in our faces." Majors was dejected to be so snubbed by his friend Aubry, but when he arrived in Santa Fe he was told of Aubry's plan for a record ride. "It was," wrote Majors, "the supreme effort of his life." The mare, Dolly, was "one of the finest pieces of horse flesh I ever saw." [20]

There were no Indian attacks, but nature made the trip miserable. It rained for twenty-four consecutive hours, and for nearly six hundred miles the trail was muddy. Many swollen streams also delayed him. He had to stop to transact business at Fort Mann, and had messages to deliver to several companies of troops on the trail.

He broke six horses during the ride, walked twenty miles, slept two and a half hours, and ate only six meals. Aubry reached Independence in the evening of September 17, "his foaming horse half ran, half staggered."

[20] Majors' reminiscences are in the *Kansas City Globe,* Feb. 10, 1890. Majors also mentioned the incident in his *Seventy Years on the Frontier,* pp. 185-87; "There is perhaps not one man in a million who could have lived to finish such a journey."

LT. GEORGE BREWERTON
This traveling companion of
Kit Carson interviewed Aubry on the
trail in 1848, commenting on the
similarity between Aubry and Carson.
From *Harper's Monthly*, Sept. 1862

ALEXANDER MAJORS
Majors was the only man to leave an
eyewitness account of Aubry's famous
ride from Santa Fe to Independence in
five and one-half days.
Courtesy, Natural History Museum, Los Angeles

ARKANSAS CROSSING
The major ford on the Santa Fe Trail crossed this river.
From *Harper's Monthly*, Sept. 1862

INDIAN ATTACK ON AUBRY'S CARAVAN
The threat of attack was always present, though for Aubry the danger
was greatly magnified on his solitary dashes across the plains.
From Tassé, *Les Canadiens*, II

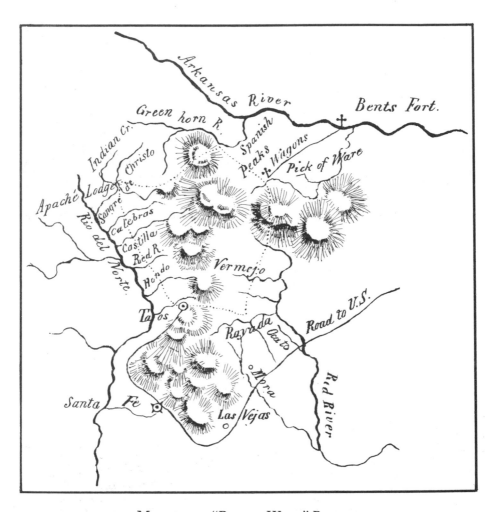

MAP OF THE "PICK OF WARE" RESCUE
The route of Major Beall and his troops for the relief of Aubry's
beleaguered caravan is shown as a dotted line. The "Pick of Ware"
is more commonly called the Purgatoire. Several of the geographic
names are misrepresented on this 1850 map.
From House Executive Document 17, 31st Cong., 1st sess., 1850

Aubry had to be helped from his horse; a few accounts mentioned that his blood had caked him to the saddle.[21]

For the ride Aubry had used the dragoon saddle, devised by Thornton Grimsley of Saint Louis. The Grimsley was a lightweight saddle which in a few years would be widely adopted by Confederate, and some Union cavalry. Aubry claimed that "the Chihuahua, San Juan, New Mexico, or English saddle is not to be named in comparison. . . Mr. A. considers it the *ne plus ultra.*" Such an endorsement by the best rider on the plains must have had an effect on the sale of Grimsley saddles.[22]

This has remained the world's most remarkable long distance ride: 780 miles in five days and sixteen hours, or as Aubry phrased it, 190 miles to the twenty-four hours. Frank Dobie wrote: "The legends of the Tartars and Scythians do not recall its equal."[23] Aubry's contemporaries used him as a measure of accomplishment. For example, Spruce M. Baird from Santa Fe wrote to the governor of Texas in December of that year about various travel distances and times; he hoped that the speed to Chihuahua could be shortened as "Mr. Aubry of this place" did on the trip to Missouri.[24]

Never again would Aubry attempt such a ride, but there was no need to do so. To this day no one has come close to breaking the distance-speed record. Twelve

---

[21] The best contemporary account of the ride is in *Daily Missouri Republican,* Sept. 23, 1848; see also *Daily Reveille,* Sept. 24 & 26, 1848. Abner Adair, who would later ride with Aubry, was in Independence at the time of the arrival; his reminiscences are in the *Odessa Democrat* (Mo.), Feb. 23, 1917. A good summary of the ride is in Bieber, *Exploring Southwestern Trails,* pp. 47-48.   [22] *Daily Reveille,* Sept. 26, 1848.

[23] Dobie, *Southwest Review,* XIII (1928), 135.

[24] Baird to Wood, Dec. 18, 1848, Santa Fe Papers, Tex. St. Lby., Austin.

years later the creators of the Pony Express system
would remember Aubry's ride, in particular his scheme
of having ready mounts stationed along the route. Alexander Majors, who witnessed the Aubry record ride,
was one of the founders of the Pony Express. One historian of the Pony Express wrote that Aubry's ride was
the "greatest physical achievement of all performances
of the horsemen of the West." [25]

The number and positions of the relay stations set up
by Aubry are not clear. He had at least five stations, one
at Fort Mann. Because he started astride Dolly, who
was good for about two hundred miles, it appears that
he was more concerned with the later legs of the journey
than the first. Also, the most dangerous Indians were the
Jicarilla Apaches, who were most threatening in the
vicinity of Santa Fe and Las Vegas. Farther on, the
Pawnees and Comanches could be a threat, but their
attacks were more sporadic than those of the Apaches.

As dramatic as the ride was, and though the people
of the country were amazed by Aubry's deed, the man
– and the record – have passed into obscure history.
Around Missouri there is still an occasional newspaper
article or mention of the ride in an historical journal,
but Aubry's quest for enduring fame seems to have been
a failure.[26]

After arriving in Independence, Aubry was carried
into the finest hotel in town, the Noland House, where

---

[25] William L. Visscher, *The Pony Express,* pp. 38-39.

[26] A few articles over the years have been "Famous Rides of the West,"
New York Times Magazine, Apr. 1, 1928; "F. X. Aubry Made Famous Ride
from Santa Fe 92 Years Ago," *Independence Examiner,* Oct. 11, 1940; "Before
He Was 20, F. X. Aubrey Blazed to Fame," *Kansas City Times,* Sept. 12,
1964; Roger Sheldon, "Plainsman in a Hurry," *Old West,* II (Winter 1965),
43, 58.

he ate a quick meal of ham, eggs, and coffee. Before
going to bed he left instructions with the genial proprietor, Smallwood Noland, to wake him after three
hours; six hours later he was awakened, and he fur-
iously lectured the proprietor, explaining that he was
used to taking his food and rest in broken doses. Poor,
perplexed Noland had to put up with a tongue-lashing
because he was being considerate towards the exhausted
rider.[27]

From Independence Aubry boarded the steamer *Ber-
trand,* but en route he was delayed for hours by fog and
low water on the Missouri river. He got off at Saint
Charles, hired a buggy, and arrived in Saint Louis in
the evening of September 22, ten days after leaving
Santa Fe, a distance of 1,200 miles. The editor of the
Daily Missouri Republican wrote:

> Yesterday evening we were very much surprised to see in our
> sanctum Mr. F. X. Aubrey, direct from Santa Fe. If an appari-
> tion had sprung up, it would not have astonished us more, for it
> was but the other day we bade him good bye on his way out.[28]

The editor of the Santa Fe newspaper had written a
letter which was hand-delivered by Aubry to the editor
of the Saint Louis *Daily Reveille,* which began: "Allow
me to introduce you to the man to whom the telegraph
is a fool." The *Reveille,* after outlining Aubry's exploits, claimed that the ride "transcends the history of
travelling."[29]

---

[27] Details differ a bit in the two accounts based on eye-witnesses; Adair in
Odessa Democrat, Feb. 23, 1917, and Tassé, *Les Canadiens,* II, p. 190. The
Noland House is briefly described in *Daily Missouri Republican,* June 3, 1849;
Mr. Smallwood Noland was "a perfect gentleman . . . full of fun and
witicisms."

[28] Issue of Sept. 23, 1848.   [29] Issue of Sept. 24, 1848.

This trip, of course, there was no "journal." Although Aubry had strapped himself to the saddle for the ride, so he could sleep without falling off, he was still the observant plainsman. He kept mental notes on water and grass conditions, remembered all the military units and officers that he passed on the trail, and delivered recent Santa Fe newspapers to several Missouri editors.[30] This was not merely a backwoods game to pass the time on the road. Aubry's news of Santa Fe, and the trail, was later published in the *Niles' National Register*.[31]

Pushing the glory temporarily aside, Aubry at once made plans for a third trip to Santa Fe in the same year. By September 25, a few days after his hero's welcome in Saint Louis, he had finished purchasing a large stock of goods and had it shipped to Independence. He left the following day for western Missouri, carrying with him the Santa Fe mail.[32]

Aubry left Independence on October 8 with "a large stock of merchandise," but the number of wagons is unknown. Traveling with Aubry was Spruce M. Baird, recently appointed "judge" of Santa Fe "County," by Texas Governor George T. Wood in an effort to annex New Mexico Territory to Texas.[33] Baird was to praise Aubry's trail skills and would play a role in the last chapter of Aubry's career.

On October 21, at Cow Creek, Aubry learned of a recent Jicarilla Apache attack near Las Vegas, New

30 *Daily Reveille,* Sept. 24, 1848.   31 Issue of Oct. 4, 1848.
32 *Daily Missouri Republican,* Sept. 26, 1848; *Daily Reveille,* Sept. 26, 1848; *New York Daily Tribune,* Feb. 28, 1849.
33 Barry, *Beginning of the West,* pp. 780-81.

Mexico, where several hundred horses and mules were run off. Forty-six of the stolen mules had belonged to Aubry, who usually kept animals there. Shortly after hearing of the Indian menace to come, and while still near Cow Creek, the Aubry train was attacked by Indians. Some of the mules were stolen, and a stockherder named Williams was killed.[34]

Mules were not only necessary for Aubry, they were costly. Mules sold from $60 to $75 at this time, and because of the large number of traders and increasing numbers of emigrants, both mules and oxen were in short supply. One estimate during this era indicated that the cost of keeping a mule was $275 a year (grain, medicine, wagon master, farrier, etc.).[35]

The Indian attacks had become so numerous on the trail that Lieutenant Colonel William Gilpin and troops were assigned to keep the trail open west of Fort Mann. Gilpin had at least moderate success, as Ceran St. Vrain and William Bent, well-known travelers on the trail, felt that Gilpin's presence "had a very happy effect upon the Indians in that country." Gilpin had succeeded in "intimidating the most formidable bands of the prairies." Yet the need for soldiers on the trail meant that merchants traveling in small groups would still be in danger of attack, as troops were not plentiful enough to escort the many caravans of traders

[34] For attack on Aubry train see *Daily Missouri Republican,* Nov. 14, 1848. For summary of entire trip see Walker D. Wyman, "F. X. Aubry: Santa Fe Freighter, Pathfinder, Explorer," *New Mex. Hist. Rev.,* VII (Jan. 1932), p. 4, and Barry, *Beginning of the West,* p. 780.

[35] *Weekly Reveille,* Apr. 16, 1849. See also Report of Captain L. C. Easton in U.S., Senate Exec. Doc. 1, *Annual Report, Secretary of War,* 32nd Cong., 1st sess. (1851), p. 241.

and emigrants. Unlike the glory days of the Mexican
War, Gilpin now commanded a collection of recent
immigrants from Europe and city boys who, according
to Gilpin's biographer, should never have left Fort
Leavenworth. His Mounted Missouri Volunteers (or
Santa Fe Trace Battalion) were not crack troops, but
they were still a welcome sight to merchants on the
trail.[36]

Anxious because of the Indian threat and the increasing cold and snow, Aubry pushed the caravan faster,
this time going via Bent's Fort route, rather than the
more familiar Cimarron cut-off through the *Jornada
del Muerto*. On November 11, near Bent's Fort, Richard Kern overtook Aubry's wagons and wrote in his
diary that Aubry's mules were "nearly given out."[37]

Approaching the Raton Pass, Aubry sped on in advance of his wagons to Santa Fe to get more forage and
additional mules. But the plainsman's luck was running
thin.[38]

About December 1, before dawn, Aubry awakened
the territorial governor, Lieutenant Colonel John M.
Washington. According to the only account of this
meeting, Aubry gave the governor an ultimatum:
"Governor, I have 400 men, 1200 mules and much merchandise in danger in the Rockies; I'll lose it without
immediate help from your troops." The governor hesitated, said he needed time to reflect on such a move.
Aubry replied: "Governor, I need help now, if you

[36] *Daily Reveille*, June 3, 1848, for St. Vrain and Bent comments. See also
Thomas L. Karnes, *William Gilpin, Western Nationalist*, pp. 187-211.

[37] Diary of Richard Kern in LeRoy R. Hafen (ed.), *Frémont's Fourth Expedition: The Disaster of 1848-1849*, p. 116.

[38] Account in *New York Tribune*, Feb. 28, 1849; also summarized in Wyman, *New Mex. Hist. Rev.*, VII (1932), 4.

refuse me, I will take extreme means to get help." Supposedly the governor, who knew Aubry, decided to act.[39]

Whether or not the above conversation took place, action did follow. Major Benjamin L. Beall, with the First Dragoons, was in Santa Fe at the time, having just brought in some Apache prisoners from Taos. Within a few days he set out against Indians "in the vicinity of Red River, or the Piquet Ware." Aubry left at once with fifteen men, but when he got as far as the Red River seven men deserted (combination fear of Apaches and snow), and he was forced to turn back to Santa Fe.[40]

The crippled caravan finally came in, but seventy-five mules froze to death, and roving bands of Jicarilla Apaches ran off another seventy-five. Much of the merchandise was lost or destroyed, but Aubry was also carrying a considerable amount of wheat, and this was salvaged.[41]

Another traveler, Lieutenant Edward Fitzgerald Beale, United States Navy, had been caught in the same storm while en route from Fort Leavenworth to California, via Santa Fe. At some points the snow was twenty feet deep. He reported that "Mr. Aubrey lost 160 mules in one night from cold, and his favorite sad-

---

[39] Tassé, *Les Canadiens,* II, pp. 201-02; Aubry had "a menacing air" during the conversation.

[40] Account of the Beall expedition in *Daily Missouri Republican,* Feb. 13, 1849, and *Daily Reveille,* Feb. 14, 1849. See also a map, "Plan of the Route of the Expedition of Major Beall, 1st Dragoons for the Relief of the Wagons of Mr. F. X. Aubrey Against the Apache Indians," in U.S., House Exec. Doc. 17, 31st Cong., 1st sess. (1850). The Piquet Ware (Pick of Ware, Purgatoire, etc.) was also called the Red River. This was a branch of the Arkansas; another Red River is east of Santa Fe.

[41] *New York Daily Tribune,* Feb. 28, 1849; Tassé, *Les Canadiens,* II, p. 202; Wyman, *New Mex. Hist. Rev.,* VII (1932), 4.

dle mule was frozen to death in a tent, with two blankets on him." [42]

The effort that Major Beall had made on Aubry's behalf would not be forgotten. Lieutenant Colonel John Washington had been appointed civil and military governor of New Mexico in mid-1848, but the people of the territory thought he was too reflective and indecisive. In the following months Beall was frequently on the attack against Apaches, whereas Governor Washington continued to hesitate. The Santa Fe merchants wanted an "Indian fighter" as governor, and in the following summer Aubry, William Messervy, William Agney, and other merchants tried unsuccessfully to have Major Beall appointed. [43]

The last trip of 1848 almost wiped out Aubry, but he had accomplished all of what he had set out to do. He had shown that not only two, but three trips to Santa Fe were possible in a single season, if one were brave enough to face the uncertainties of winter. No one, except Aubry, would try this again.

And no one, to this day, has tried to equal the riding dash which enabled him to go almost eight hundred miles in less than six days. Though low on funds, because of his reputation he had unlimited credit at merchant houses in Santa Fe, Saint Louis, and Philadelphia. He was famous and successful, an unusual circumstance for a twenty-five-year-old native of Quebec on the Rocky Mountain frontier.

[42] Lieutenant Beale's account appeared in the San Francisco *Daily Alta California,* Mar. 29, 1849.

[43] For example of dislike of Washington see *Daily Missouri Republican,* May 17, 1849. For petition favoring Major Beall, signed by Aubry and a few dozen other merchants, see *ibid.,* Aug. 25, 1849.

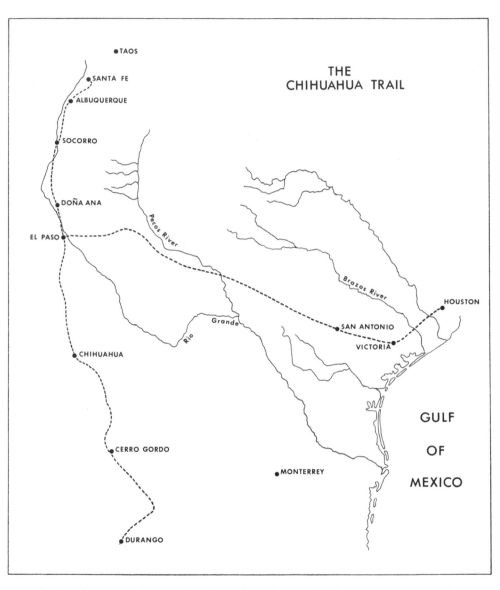

THE
CHIHUAHUA TRAIL

At first Aubry felt that the Louisiana-San Antonio-El Paso route would replace
the Santa Fe Trail, but Indian problems and low profits changed his mind.
From Webb, *Adventures in the Santa Fe Trade*

⚹ V ⚹

A Look South

Santa Fe was the wintering spot for Aubry after the disaster of December 1848. John Charles Frémont, another famous pathfinder, had also suffered from the severe fall storms. His exploring party had set out from Missouri in October. By Christmas the Rocky Mountain snow and cold had led to their miserable stop at "Camp Desolation," which was followed by many hardships, starvation, and a few deaths. Frémont eventually found refuge and comfort at the ranch of his favorite guide, Kit Carson, outside of Taos, New Mexico. Ceran St. Vrain and Aubry visited Frémont in late January; St. Vrain would leave for Saint Louis soon, so he acted as courier for Frémont. After the visit, Aubry returned to Santa Fe.[1]

By this time Aubry had heard much of the trade in Texas and Chihuahua, but he had never been there. In mid-February Aubry, Charles White, and several wagons set out for Chihuahua. They were accompanied as far as Socorro (sixty miles south of Albuquerque) by Frémont. On February 24, 1849, from Socorro, Fré-

---

[1] Frémont to Jessie Frémont, Jan. 27, 1849, in Hafen, Frémont's *Fourth Expedition,* p. 206; letter also in *Daily Missouri Republican,* Apr. 23, 1849.

mont wrote to his father-in-law, Senator Thomas Hart
Benton of Missouri:

> I must bring to your attention our fellow citizen of St. Louis,
> Mr. F. X. Aubry; you recall that he is the one who made an ex-
> traordinary trip from Santa Fe to Independence. We have been
> travelling together from Santa Fe to this place. Among other acts
> of kindness, I received from him a loan of $1,000, to purchase
> animals for my journey to California.[2]

The Chihuahua trade interested Aubry for two reasons: he was an experienced frontier merchant, yet had
never been to Chihuahua, and he felt that his early start
would place him there before other traders coming
down from Missouri.

The Santa Fe trade, as mentioned above, was actually
misnamed, because most of the merchants went farther
south: lower New Mexico, El Paso, Chihuahua, and
points beyond. Chihuahua was really the center of an
enormous trade network, with Santa Fe to the north and
Mexico City to the south. This route was El Camino
Real, a King's Highway stretching almost two thousand
miles. To the west and south of Chihuahua were other
important centers: Mazatlan, Guaymas, Durango, and
Zacatecas.[3]

During the Mexican War, United States merchants
had dominated the Chihuahua market, as many Mexican ports were closed. These merchants usually entered
Chihuahua, rented a store or used a site on the main
plaza, and sold their goods wholesale. This was Aubry's

---

[2] Letter in Charles W. Upham, *Life, Explorations and Public Services of
John Charles Frémont,* p. 298, and in Tassé, *Les Canadiens,* II, p. 192.

[3] These paragraphs are based on Max L. Moorhead, *New Mexico's Royal
Road: Trade and Travel on the Chihuahua Trail,* pp. 3, 76-77, 82, 95, 116.

normal method of operation, as it eliminated a need for a building and allowed him to make more trips back to Missouri for merchandise.

Bands of Apaches were ravaging parts of Chihuahua and Durango during the spring, and for a while rumors circulated that Aubry, White and party had been killed. This news was passed on because Aubry went through Sand Hills shortly after a Mexican caravan had been attacked; they lost five men and much of their merchandise. The rumor was put aside after Aubry reached Chihuahua safely and sent the latest news back to Santa Fe and Saint Louis.[4]

The Chihuahua trip was not very profitable for Aubry, nor for other traders. In addition to the Indian problems, the market had constricted considerably. Unlike the bonanza days of 1846-1848, the Mexican ports were no longer blockaded, so Chihuahua merchants did not have to rely on goods from the north. Furthermore, Mexican authorities had once again imposed high duties on freight coming into Chihuahua overland. The news sent in by Aubry contained the following assessment: "Trade here is very dull, and every thing with a tendency to decline."[5]

The Mexican officials in Chihuahua had more than business problems on their minds. Americans, especially Texans, were crossing Chihuahua on their way to California, and violence and murder were commonplace. The Mexican residents had been disarmed in the Mex-

[4] *Daily Missouri Republican,* May 17, 1849; St. Louis *Daily Reveille,* May 17, 1849.

[5] Wyman, *Kansas Hist. Quar.,* I (1931-32), 17-27; quote from *Daily Missouri Republican,* May 17, 1849.

ican War, so Chihuahua Governor Angel Trias began distributing arms and ammunition to control "the offensive demeanor of the foreigners." [6]

By early June, Aubry was back in Santa Fe. His fame was such that strangers in town wanted to have a look at the plainsman, as a sort of a western curiosity. William Chamberlain was passing through town on June 10 and recorded in his diary: "Saw Mr. Aubrey, a merchant of this place, the man that rode from Santa Fe to Independence, a distance of 800 miles, in 5 days and 10 hours. He is a French Canadian." [7]

In the same month Aubry became entangled in a dispute with a leading Santa Fe resident that caused him many problems. Joseph Nangle ("Don José") was a man-about-town, with a finger in every available purse. Nangle had drifted into Santa Fe early during the war and served as a private in the New Mexico Mounted Volunteers. He had a general store on Main Street, was the *Alcalde* (Justice of the Peace), and gradually convinced territorial officials that he was the foremost building contractor around. [8]

Nangle had gotten into financial trouble in May of 1848 and borrowed more than $2,000 from Aubry, promising to repay him within seven months. [9] The

---

[6] *Daily Reveille,* Aug. 29, 1849.

[7] Lansing B. Bloom (ed.), "From Lewisburg (Pa.) to California in 1849 [Notes from the Diary of William H. Chamberlain]," *New Mex. Hist. Rev.,* xx (Jan. 1945), 55.

[8] *El Republicano,* Dec. 25, 1847, notice of business establishment; *Santa Fe Republican,* Nov. 13, 1847, adv. Nangle documents of 1847, signed as *Alcalde* of Santa Fe, and Nangle contracts to build the territorial capitol are in the William Ritch Papers, Boxes 6 & 10, Huntington Lby., San Marino, Calif. The *Santa Fe Republican* of Dec. 25, 1847, reported that Nangle "is doing the best business of any merchant in town."

[9] Nangle promissory note of May 1, 1848, in Loose Diocesan Records, Arch. of the Archdiocese of Santa Fe, microfilm in State Records Center, Santa Fe.

months, and more months went by, but Nangle didn't
come up with the money. This, of course, was foreign
to Aubry; he had lent many sums to others, and also
had borrowed heavily from friends and business houses
from Santa Fe to Philadelphia. The gentleman's code
was always followed, and the loans were repaid.

So Aubry, convinced that Nangle was a scoundrel,
approached him for a final try in the Plaza of Santa Fe
on June 29, 1849, again without results. Then Aubry,
"with force and arms with and upon Joseph Nangle did
unlawfully make assault with a deadly weapon," a
pistol. Friends of both men broke up the encounter, and
Aubry was taken to court the next day. James Collins, a
prominent merchant, active in political affairs, and a
great admirer of Aubry, witnessed the encounter.[10]

The trial was called for mid-July, but Aubry asked
that it be postponed because witnesses George Peacock
and Benjamin Latz were absent; Aubry had not known
that their testimony would be needed.[11] The Aubry-
Nangle relationship evolved into a legal circus, as
Aubry brought suit against Nangle for nonpayment of
debt. Nangle succeeded in having the debt trial trans-
ferred to an adjacent county (Rio Arriba); he was then
busy impressing Judge Charles Beaubien with his good
manners and prompt attendance in court. Aubry never
showed up, as Nangle had planned that the case would
be called while Aubry was away on trading trips.

The territorial Supreme Court was asked to rule on
the confusions of the case. By that time, though, the

---

[10] Territory *v.* F. X. Aubry, bill filed June 30, 1849, First Judicial District,
Santa Fe County (records in the County Courthouse).

[11] Criminal Cases, No. 4, First Judicial District, Santa Fe County; Aubry
statement signed July 17, 1849.

issue had become Aubry's pistol-waving assault on
Nangle, and Aubry never received payment of the
$2,000 loan.[12] William Messervy, a leading Santa Fe
merchant and later Secretary of the Territory, shared
Aubry's opinion of Nangle. In 1853 he rejoiced that
"Nangle will have no further opportunity of handling
Public money." Messervy included Nangle in his "old
set of leaches."[13]

Aubry left Santa Fe for Independence on July 21,
1849, with a few wagons, thirteen Americans, seven
Mexicans, and 120 mules. They were attacked several
times by Apaches and Pawnees, but the party suffered
no losses. In a night attack at Ash Creek, the Pawnees
scattered shots for two hours, wounding a few mules
and riddling the wagons. Aubry and group arrived in
Independence on August 23.[14]

In the summer of 1849 many wagon trains were attacked. The Santa Fe end of the trail was particularly
vulnerable. Indian Agent James Calhoun in Santa Fe
complained that it was useless to send infantry after
mounted Indians; he needed a cavalry arm. Calhoun
wished to stop the many depredations, but he knew that
the Indians had reasons for the attacks. "No earthly

12 The case was called to trial Nov. 13, 1850, and Mar. 25, 1851; Records
of Rio Ariva, 1848 to 1865, in the Office of the District Court, Santa Fe County
Courthouse. See also Aubry *v.* Nangle, in *Reports of Cases Argued and Determined in the Supreme Court, Territory of New Mexico, from January
Term, 1852, to January Term, 1879,* I, pp. 115-18. The case was heard in Jan.
1854.

13 William Messervy to James J. Webb, July 30, 1853, in Ralph Bieber
(ed.), "The Papers of James J. Webb, Santa Fe Merchant, 1844-1861," *Wash.
Univ. Stud.,* Vol. XI, Humanistic Ser. (Apr. 1924), 291-94.

14 *Daily Missouri Republican,* Aug. 25, Oct. 1, 1849; Barry, *Beginning of
the West,* p. 883.

power can prevent robberies and murders, unless the hungry wants of these people are provided for, both mentally and physically." [15]

By mid-September Aubry had purchased merchandise in Saint Louis and organized a large caravan in Kansas City; he left there on September 15. Traveling with his caravan was the train of St. Vrain & McCarty, ten wagons, and James M. White, thirteen wagons.[16]

The trail predictions were encouraging: incoming travelers had reported abundant grass and water on the plains. Other recent news apparently did not disturb Aubry. There were reports of many caravans headed for Chihuahua, and the market there was said to be glutted.[17]

James White, traveling with Aubry, had opened commission and forwarding houses in El Paso and Santa Fe the previous year, with headquarters in Santa Fe. He was doing so well that he had decided to bring his family to New Mexico.[18] They would all be massacred in one of the territory's most dramatic Indian incidents.

On October 23, a week out of Santa Fe, White, his family, a few servants, about ten people in all, left the White wagons with Aubry and decided to go ahead to Santa Fe in two carriages. On the 25th, near Point of Rocks, a band of about one hundred Jicarilla Apaches attacked them, murdered White, William Callaway (an Aubry employee), Benjamin Bausman (a Negro

[15] Calhoun letters of July 29, Aug. 15, 1849, in U.S., House Exec. Doc. 17, *California and New Mexico: Message from the President of the United States,* 31st Cong., 1st sess. (1850), pp. 199-202.

[16] *Daily Missouri Republican,* Oct. 1, 1849.   [17] *Ibid.*

[18] Notice of opening of store in *Santa Fe Republican,* Aug. 9, 1848; advertisement in *El Republicano,* Aug. 15, 1848.

from Saint Louis), two Germans (also from Saint Louis), and a Mexican. Mrs. Ann White, her eight-year-old daughter, and a Negro woman servant were taken captive.[19]

Why White left the train in advance is not clear. A biographer of Kit Carson maintains that Aubry gave the family permission to go ahead, thinking that any danger of Indian attack had passed.[20] There is no precedent in Aubry's career for such a rash judgment; he, more than once, had been attacked on the outskirts of Las Vegas and Santa Fe. A more plausible explanation was that White made the decision, "as the weather was becoming cold and disagreeable for Mrs. White and child." [21] One of Aubry's trail companions, P. A. Sénécal, later reported that White believed the danger was past, "and in spite of the warnings of Aubry, set out in front of the convoy." [22] This version is not only a first-hand account, but is more consistent with Aubry's code for survival.

News of the massacre reached Santa Fe on October 29,and Aubry reached town the next morning. He at once wrote to contacts in Las Vegas, Taos, and other nearby communities, directing his friends to send out Pueblo Indians and Mexicans to negotiate with the Apaches for the return of the captive women. "The generous-hearted 'Telegraph' Aubrey, at once offered one thousand dollars as a reward for her redemption." Soon thereafter Manuel Alvarez, William Messervy,

[19] *Daily Missouri Republican,* Dec. 12 & 19, 1849; Feb. 1, 1850; *Daily Reveille,* Dec. 15, 1849.

[20] M. Morgan Estergreen, *Kit Carson: A Portrait in Courage,* pp. 199-201.

[21] *Daily Missouri Republican,* Feb. 1, 1850 (letter from New Mexico dated Dec. 1, 1849).   [22] Tassé, *Les Canadiens,* II, pp. 203-04.

and Indian agent James Calhoun joined Aubry and raised the reward substantially.[23]

What followed was much activity, and a tragi-comedy. Scouts, Indians, traders, and the army tried to find the women; communications flashed between the army, Indian agency, and clergy. A party sent out to trace down the Apaches contained two frontier experts, Kit Carson and Antoine LeRoux. Apparently jealousy over who was the best tracker led to wasted efforts.[24]

One unsubstantiated story circulated that concerned the ever-hesitant territorial governor, Colonel Washington. Apparently the army had five Apache prisoners kept at Las Vegas, and negotiations were begun to exchange them for Mrs. White and child, but Washington refused to allow the exchange.[25]

Pressure began to mount on Colonel Washington to act, as he had done "nothing, absolutely nothing." The citizens began to complain to the War Department how ineffective the army had been in the territory.[26]

Later, in November, an army search party led by Major William Grier tracked and caught up with Mrs. White and her Apache captors. Grier was well armed, carrying a piece of artillery along with him, which, a Santa Fe resident commented sarcastically, "is indispensible in New Mexican Indian warfare." Within

[23] *Daily Missouri Republican,* Dec. 12, 15, 19, 1849; for Alvarez and others, see *Daily Alta California,* June 27, 1850.

[24] There are many accounts of the White tragedy. For some varying opinion see Estergreen, *Kit Carson,* pp. 199-201; Tassé, *Les Canadiens,* II, pp. 203-04; Barry, *Beginning of the West,* pp. 884-85; *Daily Alta California,* Feb. 23, 1850; *Daily Reveille,* Dec. 15, 1849. An excellent account by Indian agent John Grenier is in the *Los Angeles Star,* June 25, 1853.

[25] *Daily Alta California,* Feb. 23, 1850.

[26] *Daily Missouri Republican,* Dec. 19, 1849.

sight of the army, the Apaches killed Mrs. White with an arrow through the heart and fled. When the soldiers reached the still-warm body they found a lady shoeless, in tattered clothing, and "literally worn to the bone." [27]

What happened to the Negro woman servant and the White child has never been determined. In 1851 some Shawnee hunters claimed that they saw a girl of that description among the Comanches, who most likely purchased her from the Apaches. This, and other reports, never led to the girl's release. The affair had been a shock to the entire frontier, but it would be several years before such attacks could be eliminated. [28]

The White incident was only one of Aubry's hardships on that trip. Just before the White party left, near the Cimarron, a heavy snow storm hit the caravan and Aubry lost twenty mules. He was also forced to *cache* two wagon loads of goods. The severity of the snow storm is further evidence that Mr. White felt the need to rush his family to Santa Fe. [29]

Adversity did not slow Aubry. He was in business in Santa Fe in November, wholesaling his goods, mostly sugar and coffee, and awaiting another shipment from Missouri. [30] He was ready to try another swing south into Texas and Chihuahua.

---

[27] *Ibid.*, Jan. 10, Sept. 13, 1851. There was much talk that some Utes had joined the Jicarilla Apaches in the attack on the White party. See for example the *New Mexican* (Santa Fe), Nov. 24, 1849.

[28] *Daily Missouri Republican,* May 26, 1851.

[29] *Ibid.*, Dec. 19, 1849; *cache* is French for a hiding place, usually a hole in the ground, covered and disguised. Proper *cache* trail methods are described in Gregg, *Commerce of the Prairies*, pp. 56-58.

[30] On Nov. 24, 1849, Aubry sold $400 worth of merchandise to a Mr. Ortiz; Read Collection, State Records Center, Santa Fe.

⚜VI⚜
Disenchantment in Chihuahua

A merchant in the Santa Fe and Chihuahua trade might make a profit on one trip a year from Missouri, but two trips usually made it a certainty. In the early days of the trade, Missouri merchants charged traders twenty to thirty percent more for goods over the Eastern wholesale prices. Many traders, irked at this practice, made their own arrangements with Eastern dealers, built warehouses on the Missouri River, and began to bypass the Missouri businessmen.

The crucial factor here, though, was speed. Philadelphia and New York merchants were not going to extend credit until a trader sold his last piece of merchandise. Instead, traders had to move goods fast, preferably by wholesale, hopefully twice a year. Of the hundreds of traders in this business, Aubry was best prepared for this type of arrangement. He never retailed. He picked his wagons, men, and animals for speed, and often left his caravan to make arrangements in advance. Although he bought from Eastern merchants, he never went there. Many of his associates, such as Dr. Connelly, the Pereas, and the Oteros made at least one trip to New York or other Eastern centers to make permanent contacts.[1]

---

[1] Above paragraphs based on Brown, "The Santa Fe Trail," pp. 38-39, and Moorhead, *New Mexico's Royal Road,* pp. 76-151.

On December 1, 1849, Aubry left Santa Fe with twenty wagons and 250 mules. He took the Camino Real as far as El Paso, then turned to the east into the relatively unknown Texas hinterlands. By this time a string of military posts had been established in central and western Texas to control roving bands of Indians and to encourage settlement. The posts were located in the trouble spots but were undermanned; one report for 1850 claimed that more than two hundred people were killed by Indians in Texas.[2]

Aubry was traveling on a route pioneered by Major Robert S. Neighbors and Dr. John S. Ford early in 1849. They had been instructed to find a good wagon road between Austin and El Paso. After accomplishing this mission, they returned to San Antonio by a slightly different route in June.[3]

Aubry's immediate destination was Victoria, Texas, which was a major settlement east of San Antonio. It is not clear, but apparently Aubry traveled with empty wagons, for while in Victoria he loaded eighteen wagons "with merchandise for the Chihuahua market."[4]

His trip on the El Paso-Victoria road had convinced Aubry that western Texas, not Santa Fe, would be the route traveled by future Chihuahua traders. Aubry was not alone in the appraisal, as trader B. F. Coons wrote from El Paso that goods could be transported from New York to El Paso or Chihuahua for twenty per cent

[2] W. C. Holden, "Frontier Defense, 1846-1860," *West Texas Hist. Assoc. Year Book,* VI (1930), 35-65.

[3] A. B. Bender, "Opening Routes Across West Texas, 1848-1850," *Southwestern Hist. Quar.,* XXXVII (Oct. 1933), 116-35.

[4] *Daily Missouri Republican,* Mar. 14, 1850, copied from *New Orleans Crescent,* Mar. 4, 1850.

less than across the plains. The Missouri reaction was near outrage: "Perhaps so; he has not yet tried it."[5]

The route question was academic. A more important consideration was whether or not the Chihuahua market could absorb the dozens of caravans headed there. In addition to Coons and Aubry, traders Henry Mayer, James Lucas, and H. Lightner were in the Chihuahua market and planned to return.[6]

Although Aubry was the darling of the press of Missouri, his sentiments did not include tendencies towards loss of profit or inefficiency. If a trade network could be developed which would bypass Missouri he would approve it, provided that it was fast and free from threats of Indian attacks.

Aubry left Victoria on February 15, 1850, and passed through San Antonio on February 27, heading for El Paso, then intending to swing south to Chihuahua. He ran into a bad snow storm beyond the Pecos River and in one night lost forty mules to the weather. He reached El Paso on April 27, then swung down to Chihuahua and sold his freight. He was back in El Paso on June 1, and in little more than a week was back in Santa Fe.[7]

During the Texas leg of the trip, between San Antonio and El Paso, Aubry had an interesting encounter with Marco's band of Apaches. Aubry later reported this to Colonel George A. McCall, who was on an in-

[5] Coons had just arrived in El Paso from Chihuahua; *Daily Missouri Republican,* Feb. 12, 1850.

[6] For list of Chihuahua traders, see *ibid.,* Mar. 26, 1850.

[7] Bieber, *Exploring Southwestern Trails,* pp. 50-51, confuses the events of January-June. Aubry loaded goods in Victoria, not in San Antonio; he went to Chihuahua *after* not before he reached El Paso. For clarification see *Daily Missouri Republican,* Mar. 14, 1850, and *St. Louis Daily Union,* June 20, 1850.

spection trip to New Mexico. Aubry had about sixty
armed men with him, which assured a friendly recep-
tion from Marco. In a discussion that followed, Aubry
suggested that the Apaches no longer kill Americans.
Marco speedily agreed; he wanted to be friendly with
the Americans. But that had nothing to do with killing
Mexicans. This shocked Aubry, but Marco replied:

> I had supposed that my brother was a man of good sense. Has he,
> then, seen between the Pecos and the Limpia enough game to feed
> 3,000 people? We have had for a long time no other food than
> the meat of Mexican cattle and mules, and we must make use of
> it still, or perish.[8]

The Limpia is a creek rising in the Davis Mountains of
west Texas and flowing east, eventually entering the
Pecos River. The Apaches were a threat to all small
caravans, and B. F. Coons stated that these Indians "had
openly declared themselves hostile to the Americans."[9]
This was not what Marco had said, but then, Marco was
facing Aubry's sixty well-armed men.

Needing more merchandise for another swing into
Chihuahua, Aubry rested in Santa Fe only a day, and
on June 12 he set out for Missouri with forty-two men,
ten wagons, and two hundred mules. Over four hundred westbound wagons were met on the trail, which
must have made Aubry's business sense anxious. There
were no major incidents on the trail, though at Plum
Buttes his men had to scare off a raid on his mules by a
party of Osages. Aubry left the caravan at Cottonwood
Creek and arrived in Independence two days later, two

8 "Col. Geo. A. McCall's Report on Affairs Relating to New Mexico," Santa
Fe, July 15, 1850, in *Report of Secretary of War,* U.S. Senate, Doc. 26, 31st
Cong., 2d sess.   9 *Daily Missouri Republican,* Feb. 12, 1850.

hundred miles away, "on the same yellow mare [Dolly] that did him such service a few years ago." The *Daily Missouri Republican,* having long ago run out of superlatives, merely wrote: "Mr. Aubry moves with almost electric speed." [10]

Aubry again provided the latest news from New Mexico and Chihuahua. He reported the discovery of gold in Chihuahua, listed the Utah depredations north of Santa Fe, commented on the promising New Mexican crops, and brought with him English and Spanish versions of the proposed constitution for the state of New Mexico.[11]

Aubry also related the strange plight of Raphael Armijo, who had been taking a small caravan to Chihuahua. The group was attacked by a band of Apaches who ran off with fifty mules. The next day the Apaches returned to Armijo's camp, and in a display of either bravado or naivete offered to sell the mules to Armijo. Not having much choice, Armijo bought them "at what in that country is considered *fair* prices."

The Indian problem was more severe than ever, and for Aubry it meant an additional burden. Previously he had confined his trading to the Santa Fe Trail, so had only that stretch to consider. Now, from the Arkansas Crossing to Santa Fe, to western Texas and Chihuahua, Indians, almost by mutual agreement, were attacking at all points. A plea from Santa Fe indeed sounded desperate: "We are left without a single friend among the numerous tribes of Indians which surround

---

[10] *Ibid.,* July 8, 1850; also summarized in Barry, *Beginning of the West,* pp. 950-51. The *Daily Reveille* referred to the arrival of Aubry, "The 'fastest man' on record;" July 9, 1850.

[11] *Daily Missouri Republican,* July 8, 1850.

us. The Apaches, Navajoes and Eutaws are now in open war with us. Daily are they committing their depredations – killing the inhabitants, and driving off stock by thousands." [12] In the summer a long newspaper article on the trail events began with this sentence: "Traders to New Mexico, it is presumed, are well informed as to depredations of hostile Indians on the caravan route to Santa Fe." [13]

The Texas frontier was also aflame, as Corpus Christi, San Antonio, and El Paso were threatened. The boldness extended to the city limits of San Antonio, where Indians stole thirty horses and mules guarded by an eight-man group of Texas Rangers. It was claimed that the Indians planned to make "a simultaneously hostile descent upon the different inhabited points on that frontier." [14]

There was no rest for Aubry in Saint Louis, as he re-stocked and went to Independence. Before mid-July he was on the way back to Santa Fe. When the Aubry caravan reached Santa Fe in mid-August he had established another trail record that would never be broken; for his round trip, he had been absent from Santa Fe seventy-seven days, which was twenty-one days less than any previous trip. [15]

The reason for speed was another trip to Texas, before severe winter storms set in. What followed in Aubry's career has been difficult to establish. He was in

---

[12] *Daily Reveille,* Mar. 31, 1850, letter from Santa Fe of Jan. 31.

[13] *Ibid.,* Oct. 3, 1850; trains belonging to Dr. Henry Connelly and William Skinner had been attacked in August.

[14] Quote from *Daily Reveille,* July 13, 1850; for more on the Indian hostilities in Texas see *ibid.,* July 17, 1850.

[15] Barry, *Beginning of the West,* p. 956.

San Antonio on November 23, 1850, but the size of his caravan and the destination of the goods are unknown. It is likely that he purchased additional supplies there and made a quick trip to Chihuahua via El Paso.

From San Antonio, Aubry wrote to Saint Louis and set Missourians' minds at ease. He admitted that he had been wrong about the usefulness of the San Antonio-El Paso route as the ideal way for the Chihuahua trade to develop. Indians were attacking at many points, and Aubry realized that the cost of freight would be less via Santa Fe than by more easterly (that is, Texan) routes. Whether the Indian menace was too great, or profits too low, is not clear. Earlier in the year Aubry had reported to several editors that Chihuahua profits had declined since the war, but he felt that the situation was only temporary. By December the "temporary" most likely shifted to "permanent" in his mind. This was Aubry's last trip to Texas and Chihuahua.[16]

Aubry, earlier than most traders, realized that the Chihuahua boom years were over. Some traders still preferred the excitement and travel, though the profit margin was thin. For example, in the spring of 1850 Alfonso Anderson from Chihuahua wrote to James Collins in Santa Fe, stating that he was soon leaving for distant Guadalajara to trade. He would be in Santa Fe in August and hoped that Collins would be interested in buying his wagons and teams.[17]

Another report, late in the year, stated that "large

---

[16] An Aubry letter to the *Daily Missouri Republican* describing trade and the route appeared on Dec. 14, 1850, signed "F. X. A." See *ibid.*, Mar. 14, 1850, for Aubry correspondence taken from the *New Orleans Crescent*.

[17] Anderson to Collins, Apr. 17, 1850, in Ritch Collection, Box 7, Huntington Lby.

demands for goods were made for the southern towns
and Chihuahua." But this report was from Independence, which did not wish to see the Chihuahua overland
trade die.[18]

Aubry had assessed the situation correctly, as trade
in Texas and Chihuahua in the next year or so declined
considerably. In 1851 grass and water were scarce
around the Limpia and the Rio Grande, and caravans
coming from central Texas headed as directly as they
could for the water of the Rio Grande. Violence, too,
caused many merchants to avoid this region. This time,
not only the Indians were censured, but also "the class
of whites known as gamblers, horse thieves and cut
throats, who form the nucleus of a world of rascality,
extending from Presidio del Norte to Santa Fe." [19]

Merchants were discouraged, also, because of the
heavy competition. In a report in September of 1851,
William McKnight, traveling from Santa Fe, counted
404 wagons en route, most of them intended for the
Chihuahua trade. McKnight also noted that prior to
his departure from Santa Fe, 120 wagons had already
arrived. The market was glutted.[20]

---

[18] *Daily Missouri Republican,* Jan. 5, 1851, report from Independence dated
Dec. 27, 1850.

[19] *Ibid.,* Aug. 29, 1851, "Further from El Paso."   [20] *Ibid.,* Sept. 7, 1851.

❧VII❧

Trail Blazing

The Santa Fe trade had boomed during the Mexican War, and after 1848 was still a way of merchant life led by hundreds of freighters, teamsters, and wagon hands, although to a lesser extent. The early helter-skelter methods became modified, though. In the first rush to get provisions to Santa Fe, even some of the military caravans went without an army escort, and some of the civilian wagon trains were inadequately armed. The persistence of the Comanches, Kiowas, and Apaches convinced the merchants that only large, armed caravans would survive.

By 1850, Aubry had arranged for a doctor to accompany most of his caravans. Aubry also had an understanding with his men that if any of them lost their lives along the trail, Aubry would see to it that the men's families would receive wages, and more. Care of stranded travelers and others in distress became part of the trail code, and Aubry in particular was widely known for his gifts of food, repair of broken wagons, and other acts of kindness along the way.[1]

By 1848 merchants had worked out a code for con-

[1] Tassé, *Les Canadiens,* II, pp. 195-96.

ditions on the trail; the code would either be sent ahead
to guide oncoming trains, or to the rear to help those
following. For example, in late October of 1848, Solomon Sublette met Kit Carson near Rock Creek, and a
few days later he met Aubry at Lower Cimarron
Spring. They exchanged codes; for example, Red River
was A, C, X (A–water; C–grass; X–buffalo chips). Another useful item that was codified was wood (B). Such
codes, though, were good for only a week or so at a
time, as a dry spell, or uncommonly large numbers of
caravans could alter quantities of grass, wood, and so
forth.[2]

Although trade had leveled off a bit, movement West
had increased as thousands of settlers gathered in Missouri, made up caravans, and headed across the plains.
One estimate for 1850 placed the number headed West
at fifty thousand. St. Joseph, Missouri, became the main
jump-off point for settlers, but the Santa Fe trade still
left primarily from Independence and Westport (Kansas City).[3]

Travelers to and from New Mexico and other Southwestern points preferred to accompany Aubry's caravans. A list of those who went with him reads like a
Who's Who of the West: territorial governors, judges,
missionaries, teachers, doctors, editors, military personnel, and bankers. There were many reasons for preferring Aubry: he pushed his caravans faster than any
other freighter, he was known throughout the West for
his hospitality and fair play, and although pestered and
attacked on many occasions by Indians, the Aubry car-

2 Solomon Sublette Papers, folder 1848, Missouri Hist. Soc., St. Louis.
3 St. Louis *Weekly Reveille,* June 3, 1850.

avans made their destinations. The only tragedy had
been that of the White family, who met death not because they traveled with Aubry, but because they left
Aubry's wagon train. *presumably*

By the early 1850s Aubry had collected some outstanding trail bosses. His stalwarts were young Dick
Williams and William Baskerville, and his servant
Pompey. In later years the trail bosses, and all of the
hands, would relate that the happiest, most exciting
time of their lives was while serving with the Aubry
caravans.

Although money and Aubry were close friends by
1850, he always needed some new challenge to make
life interesting. His speed records were unbreakable,
and other merchants shied away from trying so many
trips in one season. So, Aubry decided to improve his
reputation and make life easier for himself and other
traders by finding a shortcut on the Santa Fe Trail.

The Cimarron Cut-off, which connected the Cimarron and Arkansas Rivers, had been in use since the
early 1820s. This was a seventy-mile stretch through
sand hills with no water and little vegetation. This
jaunt was known as the *Jornada del Muerto* (Road of
Death).[4] The other way to Santa Fe, via Bent's Fort
and Raton Pass, was about one hundred miles longer,
but it had adequate water and more wood and vegetation. What Aubry sought, then, was a way to avoid both
the *Jornada del Muerto* and the longer Raton Pass
route.

Captain Randolph Marcy, who had often crossed the
Jornada, considered it treacherous but manageable. In

---

[4] Gregg, *Commerce of the Prairies*, pp. 238-41.

his guide for beginners, Marcy suggested traveling during the night and resting at daylight while the oxen and mules grazed for a few hours; hopefully there would be dew on the grass. Travel would then continue until the heat of noon, rest until late afternoon, then commence night travel again. It was this reliance on chance finding of grass and water that Aubry wished to avoid.[5]

On March 10, 1851, Aubry left Independence with a large caravan. About a week later he met an old friend, Major Francis Cunningham, at Lost Spring, coming east. Cunningham passed on the normal account of which bands of Arapahoes and Apaches Aubry might meet. Without any major problems, Aubry arrived in Santa Fe in mid-April, the first trader to arrive that season.[6]

Even on the road, Aubry had been developing his plan for a new route on the return trip. He told travelers on April 5, a few days out of Santa Fe, that he would leave as soon as possible and would reach Independence about mid-May. "He proposes, we presume, to make another of his very rapid journies." [7]

The census of New Mexico had just been taken by C. H. Merritt, traveling with Major Cunningham, and in the entire Territory of New Mexico there were 61,574 inhabitants, including 650 "Americans." [8] Yet merchants feared the Santa Fe market was about to crash. The army had a fine post in Santa Fe, Fort Marcy, but a plan was being discussed to remove all

---

[5] Randolph Marcy, *The Prairie Traveler,* pp. 52-54.

[6] *Daily Missouri Republican,* Mar. 12, 1851; see *ibid.,* Apr. 28, 1851, for Aubry at Whetstone Branch on Apr. 5.   [7] *Ibid.,* Apr. 28, 1851.

[8] Census is summarized in *ibid.,* Mar. 31, 1851.

troops from the city, to an undetermined site miles northeast of town. This would have a great impact on sales and life in Santa Fe.

The lack of law and order in Santa Fe at this time is difficult to exaggerate. What follows is a typical comment on garrison life in the city:

> It is disgusting to witness the daily scenes of drunkeness and debauchery which are constantly passing before your eyes – soldiers reeling and staggering through the streets, grinding their tortuous way from one den of infamy to another – broils at every grog shop in town, and every species of rumpus, riot and row kicked up almost every night at the low fandangoes which are the places of unfailing resort to the soldiers in garrison.[9]

Even normally peaceful pursuits in New Mexico often led to violence. In the election in the autumn of 1851, in Bernalillo County, three men were killed in an argument over merits of candidates: "God knows where it will end." Events of this nature led the *Daily Alta California* to state: "A fearful state of society is said to exist in New Mexico. Crime of the deepest dye stalks through the land." [10]

There was little time for Aubry to consider the future of Santa Fe on this trip. He quickly disposed of his goods for wholesale prices at the Plaza, and on April 23 he left Santa Fe with his wagons for Missouri; there were three inches of snow on the ground at the time. Near Cold Spring, in the modern Oklahoma Panhandle, he left the trail to look for a new route.[11]

---

[9] *Daily Missouri Republican,* Jan. 10, 1851, report from Santa Fe dated Nov. 22, 1850.

[10] *Ibid.,* Oct. 3, 1851; *Daily Alta California,* Dec. 10, 1851.

[11] Much of what follows is based on new evidence gathered by Leo Oliva in "The Aubry Route of the Santa Fe Trail," *Kansas Quar.,* v (Spring 1973), 18-29. The map on page 106 is also drawn from this source.

At first the travelers found water and grass, but the next day they crossed thirty-five miles without seeing any water, wood, or grass. They took time out to explore an unusual canyon, hundreds of feet deep and about fifty yards wide. However, the animals were without water, and the men had only one gallon in camp – they decided to strike out for the Arkansas River by the most direct route possible.

By the time the party reached the Arkansas River on May 3, they had been without water for two days and had traveled through sand and hot sun. They were so desperate for water that they drank antelope blood.[12]

A day later, the Aubry party passed thirty lodges of Cheyennes, who were on their way to Fort Mackay (soon thereafter called Fort Atkinson, west of modern Dodge City). The next day, at the fort, Aubry saw a congregation of Comanches, Cheyennes, Arapahoes, Kiowas, and Apaches, who were sitting in council with Lieutenant Colonel William Hoffman. Both sides of the river were crowded with lodges for about fifteen miles. Aubry had arrived just after the smoking of the peace pipe; he reported that Colonel Hoffman was acting with prudence, and that there was a good chance for peace on the plains, except with the Comanches and Apaches.[13]

In a burst of speed reminiscent of earlier days, Aubry left his wagons near Cottonwood Crossing and raced two hundred miles to Independence in two days, having made the entire trip from Santa Fe in nineteen days. He arrived in Independence on May 12, exhausted and disappointed at not discovering a good shortcut.[14]

[12] *Daily Missouri Republican,* May 19, 1851, Aubry journal.
[13] *Ibid.*   [14] *Ibid.*

After a few days in Independence, Aubry and other New Mexico merchants who had been congregating there took the steamer *Kansas* and arrived in Saint Louis on May 24. "He had in his charge a map of New Mexico, which is to be forwarded to Washington City." [15]

A year later, while sipping a drink in the Planters Hotel in Saint Louis, Aubry described the trip to writer Max Greene. "There is no suffering like that of thirst," he told Greene. Aubry did not blame himself — he blamed the army map makers. According to Greene and Aubry, the topographical experts got no closer to such trails than Washington or Saint Louis, yet they eagerly noted trail positions on colorful maps. Apparently Aubry, while in Santa Fe, had studied and copied these maps and "in unsophisticated reliance" on them had made mistakes on the trail.

Greene's conclusion: "When you would pass upon the desert . . . put not your trust in maps." This was not to be Aubry's last encounter with the Army Topographical Corps. Greene was familiar with most of the important mountain men and merchants, and he referred to Aubry as "the most intrepid and fortunate in his expeditions, not excepting Mr. Christopher Carson, the Bentonian embodiment of Western romance." [16]

Danger on the trail, especially in New Mexico, was as frequent as ever. Near Santa Fe, William Skinner was murdered, apparently by Mexicans. A young clerk was pursued outside of town by eight Navajos; though severely wounded he managed to escape. The violence in the territory was many-sided, and causes had been

15 *Ibid.,* May 25, 1851.
16 Max Greene, *The Kanzas Region,* pp. 50-52.

pushed aside in favor of reprisals. Four Navajos were enticed into Cibolita, where a party of Mexicans lying in ambush murdered three of them. Also in Cibolita, a Navajo chief was whipped in public by the army officer in command there.[17]

Life on the trail, too, was uncertain and precarious. In one incident in 1851, a traveler named Rippetoe left New Mexico for Missouri with little besides a horse and rifle. He reached Fort Mackay, rested, then tried to swim the Arkansas, where he lost his horse, rifle, and ammunition. He staggered on through Arapahoe, Kiowa, and Pawnee country unnoticed and reached Missouri after eighteen days on the trail. In the same year a traveler died and was buried on Mud Creek; when later travelers passed by, the body "had been disinterred by the beasts and birds." In another incident, at the Upper Cimarron, a party set out to hunt antelope, leaving two men to guard the wagons. A group of Indians arrived, turned over the wagons, pawed the contents, and "feeling satisfied they then left without doing further damage."[18]

In late spring of 1851, Aubry was in Independence and he left for Santa Fe before the end of June, accompanied by his friend Dr. Henry Connelly, Lieutenant Colonel Dixon Miles, and a few soldiers.[19] Near Pawnee Fork the train was hit by one of the cholera outbreaks frequent during this era. Aubry and ten of his men had cholera, but only one died, a Shawnee hunter named Logan. The cholera spared no train; even the troops on the trail, who tried to bypass cholera-ridden

17 *Daily Missouri Republican*, July 27, 1851.   18 *Ibid.*, Aug. 17, 22, 1851.
19 *Ibid.*, June 29, 1851; Aubry was still at Independence a few days earlier.

caravans, were themselves stricken. By early August the cholera epidemic was said to be over; there were a few cases at Fort Mackay, "only three of which were fatal." [20]

The Aubry party lost a few days, but recovered and moved along at a decent pace. At the Arkansas Crossing Aubry wrote a letter to Independence, describing the cholera perils. He also included some astonishing news: "The Arkansas river has gone dry." Whether or not it was the season, or a change in river direction, had not been determined. [21] Aubry reached Santa Fe around August 30.

The removal of troops from Santa Fe had taken place before Aubry arrived. On July 19, Colonel F. V. Sumner announced that the headquarters and depot for the Ninth Military Department would be shifted to the Moro River (this was the origin of Fort Union). The drinking, gambling, fighting, dancing, and general rowdyism and violence caused by the soldiers convinced Colonel Sumner that the troops must be separated from the residents of Santa Fe. In addition to the loss of business to the city, many teamsters, mechanics, and other government employees were out of work. [22] No doubt Aubry, with his business awareness, sensed that his time as a Santa Fe trader was short.

Aubry began preparations at once for his return to Missouri; this time he was confident of finding the trail shortcut. He gathered his crew in Las Vegas, east of

[20] For Aubry and cholera see *ibid.*, July 25, 1851, Aug. 28, 1851; for other cholera problems on the trail see issue of July 27, 1851.

[21] *Ibid.*, Aug. 28, 1851.

[22] For details of the move, including General Order No. 17 from Col. Sumner, see *Daily Missouri Republican*, Aug. 28, Sept. 1, Nov. 6, 1851.

Santa Fe: sixty-two men, thirty wagons, and three hundred mules. They departed September 19. In the Oklahoma Panhandle they left the trail, traveled from ten to forty degrees east of north to the Arkansas, and found "an excellent wagon road, well supplied with water and grass, and avoiding the Jornada and Cimarone trail altogether." [23] Aubry had built-in proof of his success: traveling with him were several members of the United States-Mexican Boundary Commission, who vouched for the trail. Also on the trip as passengers were William Messervy, Charles Spencer, B. F. Mosely, and P. H. LeBlanc, a French Canadian from Santa Fe. Aubry kept his hand in, as two days from Independence he left the caravan and covered more than two hundred miles on his favorite mare Dolly, arriving on October 11.[24]

Impatient to prove the worth of his new trail, Aubry, with thirty wagons, set out from Westport on October 23 with his third train of the year. Traveling the regular trail along the Arkansas River to a point about sixty miles above the Cimarron Crossing, he turned south at what would be called the Aubry Crossing to start down the new Aubry Trail. On November 9, Aubry was at Fort Atkinson, where he was interviewed by the commanding officer, Captain Simon Bolivar Buckner. Aubry's enthusiasm caught Buckner, who immediately wrote to his superiors at Fort Leavenworth praising the new route and also providing a map. The advantages of the new route were numerous: more water and wood, short distances without water, only two

[23] Barry, *Beginning of the West,* p. 1015.
[24] *Ibid.,* p. 1042; Oliva, *Kansas Quar.,* v (1973), 21.

miles of sandy road, and good shelter. Buckner's post, Fort Atkinson, was responsible for protecting the Santa Fe Trail, so he was particularly pleased with the good accommodations on the Aubry Cut-off.[25]

Buckner explained Aubry's trail-finding procedure:

> The method adopted by Mr. Aubry was to direct the movement of his train by compass, until some obstacle was met which should render a change of direction necessary; or until some information was received by reports from men whom he kept at distances of several miles on both sides of his wagons.[26]

The new trail was a success. It was late in the season, there were severe storms, the weather was cold, yet Aubry reached Santa Fe in mid-December "with heavy teams and without loss of an animal." [27]

This was great news for Santa Fe, as year-round trips to Missouri now seemed possible. Also, the new route was estimated fifty miles shorter. The words for him in Santa Fe were deserved:

> His traveling enterprise and endurance exceed, perhaps, those of all other men living. . . Mr. Aubry, it is needless to say, has gained the highest admiration for his achievements, as the electric traveler. Further, he deserves great credit for his untiring effort to explore new paths, which shall facilitate the communication with New Mexico, and add to the comfort and safety of the traveler on the desert route which leads to it.[28]

The trail, although used by hundreds of travelers, has been lost to history. In the dozens of works published on the subject, there is scant mention of the Aubry Cut-

---

[25] Oliva, *Kansas Quar.,* v (1973), 21-22.

[26] Buckner to McDowell, Nov. 12, 1851, *ibid.,* p. 22.

[27] *Daily Missouri Republican,* Feb. 2, 1852, news from Santa Fe.

[28] *Ibid.,* letter from Santa Fe.

off, usually with a phrase "not generally used." [29] Yet
one scholar has recently unearthed enough evidence to
show that there was a continual, heavy use of the Aubry
Trail by merchants, travelers, and the army, through
the Civil War years.[30] Later, Fort Aubrey would be
erected in the vicinity, during the Indian tensions of the
mid-1860s.

[29] William Bernard, "'Westport and the Santa Fe Trade," *Trans. of the Kansas St. Hist. Soc.,* IX (1905-06), 562.
[30] Oliva, *Kansas Quar.,* V (1973), 25-27.

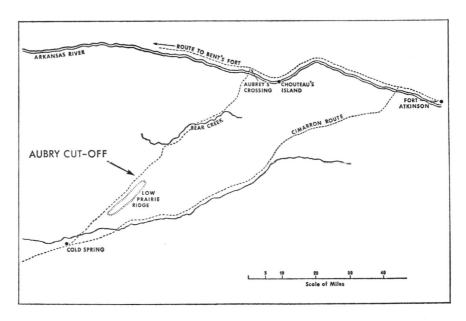

The Aubry Cut-off had more water, grass and wood
than the desert-like Cimarron route.

❧VIII❧

Farewell, Missouri

In 1852 Aubry made three trips between Missouri and Santa Fe, using the Aubry Cut-off, but boredom had set in. He was the world's fastest horseman, the trail's speediest merchant, and had discovered a new route. Also, he was rich. But as there was little more for him to excel in, he made this his last year on the Santa Fe Trail. Another factor in his decision must have been the shifting of troops out of Santa Fe to Fort Union, which greatly depressed the New Mexico market.

The "intrepid, indefatigable Francis X. Aubry" left Santa Fe on December 31, 1851, and had as guests Army Lieutenants James Ward and Charles Field. The party arrived in Independence on February 5, 1852, and Aubry was in Saint Louis on February 14; he had brought in twelve wagons and "a large amount of specie." By this time most shipments of money from Santa Fe to Missouri were carried by Aubry. He had varied his cut-off this time, crossing the Arkansas River higher up than usual. The party encountered severe cold, much ice, and almost two feet of snow, yet did not lose a single mule. They camped on Chouteau's Island and were thwarted in their search for water, as the river was frozen to the bottom. Aubry decided that his earlier cut-off was superior to this one.[1]

Winter traveling with severe cold and deep snow was commonplace for Aubry by now, but some of his new men were appalled at the conditions. According to Baskerville, on one such trip the men were complaining of the bitter cold, and Aubry "good-naturedly told them that he had been over the trail forty times, and that particular trip was the most pleasant he had ever made."[2]

In February, Aubry outfitted in Saint Louis and Independence, and he set out from Independence on March 1, again the first Santa Fe trader on the trail.[3] By this time Aubry's fame was even used by advertisers. Merchants in Kansas City publicized their wares to westward-bound travelers, claiming "Aubry, Messervy, Huston, Kit Carson, and all the celebrated voyageurs invariably select Kansas as their starting point."[4] The words were fine, but not accurate. Aubry selected Independence more than Westport (i.e., Kansas City region) for his gathering-departing point. On this trip out Aubry made a short swing to the northwest to Fort Leavenworth, where he joined several government trains headed for New Mexico.

At Fort Leavenworth occurred the only known female interest shown by Aubry, as he spent a few days courting an old friend, Eliza Sloan. She was a young widow and had known Aubry earlier on the trail during the Mexican War, when her husband was an Army

[1] *Daily Missouri Republican,* Feb. 15, 1852; Barry, *Beginning of the West,* p. 1064.   [2] Baskerville Memoir, Western Hist. Dept., Denver Pub. Lby.

[3] Barry, *Beginning of the West,* p. 1067.

[4] Advertisement in *Daily Missouri Republican* through Apr. 1852.

surgeon in New Mexico. She was going to Santa Fe with one of the government trains. Eliza had her two young children along, Marian and Will, and Aubry spent much time with the three of them.

According to Marian's memoirs, Aubry "was our very good friend. We took our childish woes to him for solace, visited him in his great covered wagon, and were treated as welcome guests." Captain Aubry enjoyed passing on some trail lore, told many stories, and seemed to enjoy teasing the widow by calling her "Lizzie."

Aubry's train left with several government trains, with which widow Sloan and family were traveling. They met almost daily on the trail, especially in the evenings. Aubry seems to have become a father figure for the children, as he "cured" earaches by blowing smoke in the children's ears, carved a willow whistle for Will, and rocked Marian to sleep by the campfire. Once he scolded the children severely for wandering too far from the wagons. In these childhood memories one gets only brief mentions of Aubry with the widow, but Marian claimed that "mother's dearest friend and most ardent admirer was Captain F. X. Aubry."[5]

After the caravans entered New Mexico Territory, Aubry announced to the Sloan family that "This is the place where only the brave and the criminal come. It is called 'The Land without Law.' " Aubry saw the family a few more times in Santa Fe but did not apparently pursue the widow. He was only twenty-eight years old at the time, and his life was so hectic and restless that he did not even have a permanent address in Santa Fe or Saint Louis.

[5] "Memoirs of Marian Russell," *Colorado Mag.,* xx (May 1943), 81-95.

Aubry reached Santa Fe early in April, and on the eleventh was back on the trail, trying to shorten the Aubry Cut-off a bit. Traveling with him was William S. Allen, Secretary of New Mexico Territory, his former wagonmaster J.-A. Sénécal, Reverend E. G. Nicolson and family, and a few other passengers. They arrived in Missouri on May 8. Much Mexican money was brought in, carried by Aubry, "the celebrated Santa Fe courier." [6]

Allen wrote an article about the trip for the *Daily Missouri Republican,* with emphasis on the Aubry Cut-off. He was impressed with the climate, geography, and water and grass supplies. Not only was the route shorter, but Aubry convinced Allen that with a bit more looking an additional one hundred miles could be shaved. Allen included a chart that noted the miles between various points on the cut-off. Allen, the number two man in New Mexico, was a powerful ally in pushing recognition of the new road.

The caravan had started east on the Santa Fe Trail to Cold Spring. From there they had angled northeast a few miles, crossed the Cimarron and Bear Creek, and finally reached the Arkansas River twelve miles above Chouteau's Island, which was about fifty-eight miles north of the Cimarron Crossing. In current geographical language, the Aubry Cut-off began in the Oklahoma Panhandle, sliced northeast through the lower east section of Colorado, entered Kansas and joined the upper branch of the Santa Fe Trail near modern Kendall, Kansas.

The Allen article took up more than a full column

---

[6] *Daily Missouri Republican,* May 15, 1852; Barry, *Beginning of the West,* p. 1093.

in the *Republican,* an indication of the interest and significance of the Aubry Cut-off to the people of Missouri. Allen finished the article with a long complaint of how the people of New Mexico were neglected by the government. Hopefully, Aubry's Cut-off would make communications faster.[7]

The Aubry Cut-off was used in early June by Major Enoch Steen and 183 recruits of the 1st Dragoons who were going to New Mexico. Steen's report on the trail was mixed, but in general positive. He was annoyed at finding watering holes "dry and destitute of water." However, one week of heat in this near-wasteland could affect water and grass supplies in extreme. Steen concluded that "on the whole, however, we were satisfied that the new route . . . is greatly to be preferred to the eastern portion of the Cimarron route."[8]

One of Steen's party, Lieutenant Colonel J. H. Eaton, also criticized the inadequate water supply but felt that the route was superior to the Cimarron Cut-off. Eaton also reported that Aubry had left a part of his personality on the trail, blazing the letter "A" on some trees near the Arkansas Crossing. At the south end, where the Aubry Trail linked with the main Santa Fe Trail, Aubry had placed a wooden guideboard for travelers.[9]

By making rapid purchases, and by keeping his trail-wise crew, Aubry was able to leave for Santa Fe before the end of May. Again, an unwanted passenger accompanied them: cholera. In early June seventeen of his men were stricken at one time, and in the following

---

[7] Allen's unsigned article in *Daily Missouri Republican,* May 18, 1852. Internal evidence, and comments in the issue of May 15, indicate that Allen wrote the article.

[8] Quoted in Barry, *Beginning of the West,* pp. 1091-92.

[9] Extracts from Eaton report in Oliva, *Kansas Quar.,* v (1973), 25.

days dozens of other hands contracted the prairie menace. Although slowed down by the disease, only one of Aubry's men died.[10]

Aubry reached Santa Fe in late July, disposed of his goods, and left for Missouri on July 31; he reached Independence on August 25 without incident, bringing in twelve wagons, two carriages, and 250 mules.[11] These were "Mexican" mules, much in demand in western Missouri where the large emigrant trains were outfitted. Both in and out, Aubry had used the Aubry Trail. When he left for Santa Fe in early September his train was overtaken by a mail party which reported that they saw Aubry crossing the Arkansas "on his own road," an acknowledgement that other travelers were giving credit to Aubry for the cut-off. The mail stage, too, used the Aubry Trail and reported plenty of wood, grass, and water.[12]

In Missouri, Aubry reported another chapter in the old steal-and-sell-back game of the plains. Apaches had attacked a party of fifteen Mexicans in the *Jornada del Muerto,* killing one man and stealing twenty oxen. An hour or so later the Mexicans again encountered the Apaches and bought the stolen oxen for one horse and three mules, "and then made peace with them." This account was from Major Jefferson Van Horne who joined Aubry at the Cimarron Crossing.[13]

An Aubry account was published in the *Daily Missouri Republican* on August 31, 1852. He described the route, travel conditions, number of Indians seen along

---

[10] Barry, *Beginning of the West,* p. 1097.

[11] *New York Daily Tribune,* Sept. 8, 1852.

[12] *Daily Missouri Republican,* Aug. 28, 1852; Barry, *Beginning of the West,* p. 1121.   [13] *New York Daily Tribune,* Sept. 8, 1852.

the way, and provided a list of caravans. Among those he met were Caysan Chouteau, out for a pleasure excursion, Governor William Carr Lane on his way to Santa Fe, Bishop Lamy, Captain Simon Bolivar Buckner, and Dr. M. Dougall.

In the summer of that year Aubry got into a frontier literary argument, this time with Captain John Pope of the Topographical Engineers. Pope, a minor hero in the Mexican War, would later become a key general for the Union in the Civil War and in the post-war West. Apparently jealous of the publicity Aubry was getting for the "Aubry Cut-off," Pope let it be known that he had discovered this route earlier, in the summer of 1851. Naturally, if Pope had been in Santa Fe, instead of at Fort Leavenworth, Aubry would have challenged him to a duel. But Aubry was also good with words. The citizens of Santa Fe laughed at Pope's claim, but Aubry wanted it a matter of record. The *Santa Fe Gazette* published an extra on July 17, 1852, containing an article by Aubry refuting Pope's claim. The *Gazette* concluded: "The probability is that civilians will generally call it Aubrey's Route, while the military will designate it as Pope's Route." [14]

The war of words was meaningless, as unknown to everyone at the time, Pope and Aubry were claiming two different routes. Pope had been directed in August of 1851 by the commander of the Ninth Military Department, Colonel Edwin Sumner, to examine the country for a better, shorter route from Fort Union, New Mexico, to Fort Leavenworth. Pope succeeded with a force of twelve men, and the route later became known

[14] I have not been able to locate a copy of this extra; quoted from Barry, *Beginning of the West*, p. 1123.

as the Fort Leavenworth Road. However, Pope's road was farther west than Aubry's, reaching the Arkansas River at the Big Timbers.[15]

When he left for Santa Fe in early September 1852, Aubry was on his last trip on the trail. This time, in addition to a large stock of goods, he was also supplying the Army: twenty-nine bales of clothing for the troops at Fort Union, for which he was to be paid $12.50 per hundred pounds.[16] He arrived in Santa Fe in mid-October.

By this time New Mexico had a new territorial governor, William Carr Lane from Missouri. Like other prominent people on the frontier, Lane was impressed with Aubry and soon claimed him as a friend and advisor. Lane wrote to his wife in November, saying that their daughter Ann might soon have a visitor in Saint Louis; the governor had asked Aubry to call on Ann during his next trip. Lane continued: "He is a French Canadian, & is quite well bred. . . He appears to be restless, when stationary, & only contented, when making those appaling journeys. A thousand miles, seem no more for him, than 100 for me."[17]

---

[15] Hdqrs., Ft. Union, July 26, 1851, to Capt. H. S. Ewell, regarding number of men to go with Pope, in Ninth Military Dept., Order, Vol. 7, p. 215, Record Group 98, Nat. Arch.; Special Order 58, Aug. 6, 1851, Hdqrs., Ninth Dept., Ft. Union, authorizing Pope to make the expedition, in Arrott Coll., Highlands Univ., Las Vegas, N.M. For good summaries of Pope's route see Oliva, *Kansas Quar.,* v (1973), 23-25, and Robert M. Utley, "Fort Union and the Santa Fe Trail," pp. 15-16.

[16] Contract signed Sept. 3, 1852, St. Louis, between Aubry and Maj. D. H. Vinton; U.S., Senate, Exec. Doc. 18, 32nd Cong., 2d sess., *Report of the Secretary of War, Showing Contracts Made . . . 1852;* see also *Daily Missouri Republican,* Oct. 24, 1852.

[17] Lane to wife, Nov. 6, 1852, in "Letters of William Carr Lane," *New Mex. Hist. Rev.,* III (April 1928), 190.

≋IX≋

To California

The whole nation was talking about the West – but not about New Mexico. The Gold Rush in California, its statehood in 1850, and the increase in population for the Pacific Coast created an excitement throughout the country. Aubry was aware of the interest, much more than most citizens. For him it represented an opportunity to take his business talents farther West. Disregarding the reported dangers, he decided to become the best trader between Santa Fe and San Francisco.

But, as usual, mere money would not satisfy him; he had to have a way to combine fortune with fame. He had a true cause, almost as though a problem had been created with him in mind.

The 1850s was the decade of the great railroad controversy. The nation was growing, having just gobbled up the entire Southwest. California was now a state, yet there was not even a good stage route between East and West. Mail still went regularly around the South American route. In Congress, in the state legislatures, and in the local press, demands for a railroad to the Pacific began to accelerate. Congress finally acted in 1853 by authorizing a series of railroad surveys to be conducted by the United States Army. Aubry anticipated this move and decided to make a trading trip to California, and on his return trip he would find, at his own expense, a better railroad route than the best that government money could buy.

Politics was a problem. In this era of sectional rivalry, the best geography would not necessarily lead to the rail-building decision. Naturally, the people in Minnesota preferred a St. Paul-Seattle route, as the people in Saint Louis hoped for a central route. And residents of the Deep South, and a few people in the Southwest, preferred the extreme southern route, the 32nd Parallel, south of the Gila River.[1] That the southern route was in the Mexican state of Sonora did not bother advocates much.

Pacific railroad dreams had first been loudly voiced by Asa Whitney, a merchant in the Chinese trade, in the mid-1840s. Whitney even got Congress to pass a memorial in 1845, suggesting a railroad from the Great Lakes to Oregon.[2] After the Mexican War, Oregon had to compete with new United States points on the Pacific Coast as possible terminals: San Diego, Los Angeles, San Francisco. And in mid-country, there were many cities boasting of obvious reasons why they should be jump-off points: New Orleans, Saint Louis, Chicago, Memphis, Duluth, and even Cairo, Illinois.

Aubry, and the people of Santa Fe, hoped that a good route along the 35th Parallel could be found; this would roughly parallel a line from Los Angeles to Albuquerque. Yet New Mexico had a territorial delegate, Major

---

[1] Lynn I. Perrigo, *Texas and Our Spanish Southwest*, pp. 189-90.
[2] Ray Allen Billington, *Westward Expansion*, pp. 642-43.

Richard Hanson Weightman, who favored the southern, or Gila route. Weightman had always been a Southerner in the traditional sense of that word (he would later join the Confederacy). New Mexico opponents of Weightman claimed that he pushed for the Gila route in order to favor his friends in El Paso, Texas. Aubry, then, was in direct opposition to Weightman, which would lead to personal disaster for both men.[3]

To pay for his exploration, plus make a profit, Aubry decided to drive sheep across the desert to California and sell them in San Francisco. There was a tremendous meat shortage in California, partly the result of the break-up of the mission system almost two decades earlier, but more importantly the result of the staggering increase in population. Because of the Gold Rush, by the early 1850s the state population had jumped from 100,000 to 380,000.[4]

For generations sheep had figured prominently in the economy of New Mexico. The Spaniards introduced sheep to the region in the early 1600s, and soon local Navajos as well as Spaniards were developing large flocks. The wool, and the meat, came with a minimum of expense, though only with much care. In the Santa Fe area there were normally year-round grasses, and a few shepherds and dogs could handle a flock of several thousand sheep.[5]

The supply and demand situation seemed clear: take

[3] For lengthy anti-Weightman articles, see *Santa Fe Weekly Gazette,* Jan. 22, Apr. 2, Apr. 9, May 22, 1853.

[4] Charles Wayland Towne and Edward Norris Wentworth, *Shepherd's Empire,* pp. 87-88.

[5] W. W. H. Davis, *El Gringo, or New Mexico and Her People,* pp. 204-06.

the New Mexico sheep to California. In 1849 Antonio José Otero sent his younger brother and Antonio José Luna with twenty-five thousand sheep across the deserts and received from $10 to $25 a head for them in California. In 1851 two other groups, one from California, the other from Santa Fe, also took sheep to the Pacific Coast, attracted by the price: purchase price in New Mexico was $2, sales price in California was $18.[6]

But the profit, like digging for gold dust, was inconsistent. In late 1851 Captain Joseph Walker traveled from California to Santa Fe to purchase sheep, but the price had risen enough to discourage him; he returned "sheepless" to Los Angeles in early December. Richard Jones tried the sheep-into-gold conversion in the same year, buying 2,400 head in Chihuahua and heading west. When he reached San Diego the number had decreased to two hundred: "The speculations in sheep, recently, have been very disastrous."[7]

In 1852 a Mr. White from New Mexico made the journey with sheep as far as the Colorado River, but an Indian attack forced him to rush to Fort Yuma for help, and Indians stole thousands of his sheep. White also reported an Apache attack on a different party from Santa Fe coming west with about seven thousand sheep – all men and animals were lost. A report of a little later suggested that the Apaches, under Chief Mangas Coloradas were very friendly, selling travelers "sheep and mules for a mere trifle."[8]

---

6 For Otero and Luna see Towne and Wentworth, *Shepherd's Empire,* pp. 87-88. See also *Daily Missouri Republican,* Apr. 28, 1851.

7 *Daily Alta California,* Dec. 19, 1851; the Jones account is in *ibid.,* Aug. 26, 1851.

8 White account in *Los Angeles Star,* Mar. 6, 1852; quote from *ibid.,* June 26, 1852.

One might reasonably ask, why sheep and not cattle? One answer, of course, is that California's nearest livestock source, New Mexico, was excellent sheep-grazing country. But even if both sheep and cattle had been available, sheep would have been the selected animal. Sheep travel faster and more regularly than cattle, especially in those intervals of little water. Also, cattle stampede more easily, especially at night, while sheep customarily seek protection of the shepherd. Across the hundreds of miles of desert and rocky terrain, more sheep than cattle would survive.[9]

The potential profit intrigued Aubry, and as usual he was willing to chance any Indian attacks. Early in November of 1852 he planned his California trip. He purchased five thousand sheep from the Navajos and gathered a crew of about sixty men. The *Santa Fe Gazette* on November 13 announced that "Maj. Aubry" would leave for California in a few days. In this era most important merchants and wagon train masters were referred to by the honorific "Captain," so the newspaper obviously believed that Aubry's importance was better reflected by the new title.

The Aubry party left Santa Fe on November 16, taking along ten large wagons, one hundred mules, and one hundred horses.[10] He had clearly charted a new course for himself; he informed the editor of the *Gazette* that if he found a good railroad route "he will not hereafter be a Santa Fe, but a California trader. Success attend him."[11]

---

[9] Edward N. Wentworth, "Meat in the Diet of Westward Explorers and Emigrants," *Mid-America*, XXIX (Apr. 1947), 75-91.

[10] *Daily Alta California*, Mar. 31, 1853.

[11] *Santa Fe Weekly Gazette*, Nov. 20, 1852.

The caravan swung south along the Rio Grande and eventually took a west southwest course directly to Tucson, pioneering a new trail that cut off about 150 miles. From Tucson he followed Cooke's Trail to the Colorado River.[12] From that location Aubry wrote a letter to the *Daily Missouri Republican* dated February 10, from the "Colorado of the West."[13]

The trip so far, wrote Aubry, was not pleasant. There was a long, difficult road, with several *jornadas* (one of 100 miles), and very little water. Yet since leaving the Del Norte they had lost only one of the flock. "It is not probable we shall retain any pleasant recollections of this trip." During the entire trip, Aubry lost only twenty-five sheep and one mule; the mule was killed for food.[14]

Before they reached the Colorado, between the Pima Indian villages on the Gila River, they came upon a camp ground with bones scattered about, probably those of eight to ten persons. There were also bits of calico dresses, and a burnt wagon. Later, in Los Angeles, Aubry tried unsuccessfully to find out about the massacred party.[15]

Beyond the Colorado River lay difficult terrain for any traveler; five thousand sheep would be an added strain. They crossed the mountainous desert, heading towards Los Angeles via the route through modern San Bernardino. In the desolate areas Aubry adopted a plan to help other travelers. When he discovered a short cut,

---

12 Bieber, *Exploring Southwestern Trails,* p. 54.
13 Issue of Mar. 25, 1853.   14 *Daily Missouri Republican,* July 4, 1853.
15 Details of the massacre in "Los Angeles News," *Daily Alta California,* Mar. 31, 1853.

he attached a bottle to a stick and placed it upright; in the bottle was a paper giving the details of the road recommended.[16]

Aubry arrived in Los Angeles in mid-March and rested a few days. The trip so far had been a success. He had also transacted some business along the way. At the new Mormon settlements near San Bernardino he sold one thousand old, lame sheep for $8,000, and received $3,000 for an unknown number of "small and broken down mules." On March 15 he set out for San Francisco.[17]

Near Monterey, Aubry visited with a former Missouri acquaintance, T. J. Barnes, who was able to tell Aubry the going rates for sheep in San Francisco: $12 to $18 a head. Barnes felt that the mules and horses in the caravan would also bring a fine price, "as they are large and of the best quality." [18]

In late April the party arrived in San Francisco and had no trouble selling the sheep. Abner Adair, who was with the group, wrote that Aubry received $10 per head for the sheep, and also "disposed of wagons and extra mules at big prices." Aubry, after expenses, made more than $70,000 on the trip. He was so enthused about his new business that he told fellow Missourian Barnes in Monterey that "he is done with the trade of New Mexico . . . and he would not thank any man to offer

[16] Tassé, *Les Canadiens,* II, p. 210.

[17] *Daily Alta California,* Mar. 31, 1853; *Daily Missouri Republican,* July 4, 1853.

[18] *Daily Missouri Republican,* July 4, 1853, letter from T. J. Barnes of Monterey to J. R. Slaughter, Independence. Aubry had started out with about 5,000 sheep, but some accounts state 3,500. The discrepancy is because Aubry sold at least 1,000 sheep before he reached Los Angeles; California newspapers, correctly, stated that he arrived with 3,500 sheep.

him 50 cents per pound for freight from Independence to Santa Fe." [19]

Although pleased with the sheep business, Aubry had no intention of ever settling in California. He wrote to Santa Fe describing the conditions in California, saying that he had seen more misery, more poor men in that state than he had ever seen before. He was saying what many other observers were reporting. The Gold Rush had attracted thousands, and a bad growing season had led to hunger and other problems. Another comment from this period is typical: "Notwithstanding the wealth of California, I think it is safe to affirm that there is not a state in the Federal Union which has proportion to population, so many poor and destitute." [20]

The main purpose of the Aubry trip to California was stated in his journal: "I set out, in the first place, upon this journey to gratify my own curiosity as to the practicability of one of the much talked-of routes for the contemplated Atlantic and Pacific railroad." He had shared his purpose with editors, politicians, and other interested parties along the way, and the entire West knew what he was trying to do. Newspapers in Santa Fe, Saint Louis, Los Angeles, and San Francisco kept their readers informed of Aubry's every move. Most people in these cities wished Aubry success, as a route along the 35th Parallel would suit them best. [21]

---

[19] Adair reminiscences in *Appleton City Journal* (Mo.), May 15, 1902. For profit on the trip see Tassé, *Les Canadiens,* II, p. 210. Quote is from Barnes letter in *Daily Missouri Republican,* July 4, 1853.

[20] Aubry letter in *Santa Fe Weekly Gazette,* May 21, 1853; quote in "From California," *Daily Missouri Republican,* Apr. 19, 1853.

[21] Aubry quote from *Santa Fe Weekly Gazette,* Sept. 24, 1853. Typical comments on Aubry's plans can be seen in *ibid.,* May 21, 1853; *Daily Missouri Republican,* July 4, 1853; *Los Angeles Star,* June 25, 1853.

❧ X ❧

Finding a Railroad

The Aubry party was organized in San Francisco, consisting mostly of men who had come west with him. There were eighteen in the group, twelve Americans and six Mexicans from Santa Fe, "Messrs. Tully, of Santa Fe, and Adair, of Independence, have joined us for a pleasure trip." Tully was a lawyer, active in New Mexico political affairs. Adair had been a fan of Aubry since he witnessed the conclusion of the famous 1848 ride across the plains. Also in the group was Pompey, Aubry's Negro servant who had been with him since 1847. Pompey, on most trips, had taken care of Aubry's personal carriage; this time he rode his own horse and served as cook for the group.[1]

The party had thirty pack mules and horses, and decided not to take a wagon. On June 20 they left for Stockton; by July 6 they were on the Kern River south of Walker's Pass. Here Aubry spent eight hours inter-

[1] Much of this chapter is based on Aubry's journal, which first appeared in the *Santa Fe Weekly Gazette,* Sept. 24, 1853. Other published versions, more easily available, can be seen in Tassé, *Les Canadiens,* II, Appendix; Bieber, *Exploring Southwestern Trails,* pp. 353-77; Wyman, *New Mex. Hist. Rev.,* VII (1932), 1-31. Tully's reminiscences appeared in the Tucson *Citizen,* May 10, 1873. For Pompey, see Adair reminiscences in *Appleton City Journal* (Mo.), May 15, 1902.

viewing famed mountain man Alexis Godey, a French Canadian who had often served as a guide for Frémont. The information obtained must have been meager, for Aubry later wrote that no one knew anything of the route he intended to follow. On July 11, 1853, the Aubry party left Tejon Pass north of Los Angeles and headed east. The *Los Angeles Star* informed its readers of the "well armed and equipped party," stating that Captain Aubry intended to find a "more direct route through the mountains than any hitherto travelled." [2]

On July 13 they began crossing the Mojave Desert, and for a few days they followed the Mojave River, which varied in depth from two feet to none. Aubry was not particularly impressed with the country, but he did find enough water and grass for the animals. The only delay was a full day of rest, because one of his men was sick.

They hit the Colorado River on July 22 near present Hoover Dam. They followed the river north five miles and selected a crossing where the river was about two hundred yards wide. They made a raft of driftwood, and began a five-day campaign to cross the river. They were bothered by Indians on the nearby heights, and it was especially dangerous when the Aubry party was split on both sides of the river. The first night beavers ate the ropes holding the raft together. They finally rafted across and got all the animals into the river, and they also reached the other side safely.

While resting on the east bank, a Mexican mule boy

---

[2] For meeting with Godey, see *Daily Missouri Republican,* Sept. 16, 1853; see also *Los Angeles Star,* July 16, 1853, for Aubry departure details. A fellow French Canadian was also a member of the party, Peter Prudom (Pierre Prud'homme).

COLORADO RIVER CROSSING
Mojaves watch on the bluffs above the river. It was at this point
that Aubry and friends were bothered by the Indians in July 1853.
From *Pacific Railroad Reports*

TEJON PASS
This well-known pass between Los Angeles and the San Joaquin Valley saw many travelers
such as Aubry make their way from the southern overland trails towards the gold fields.
From *Pacific Railroad Reports*

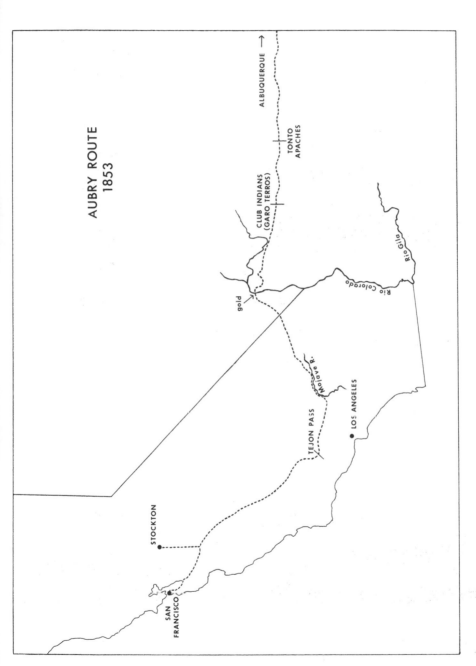

Aubry's exact routes for his two California-New Mexico trips are not known. His diaries, and the several contemporary maps, suggest that the routes for both trips closely paralleled each other. He was killed the day of his return in 1854, so was unable to add further information to the notes in his diary.

From the National Archives, RG 77

was attracted by a glistening in the sand – gold. Soon the party was "tin-cupping" and found bits of gold in every cup. On July 27, the last day on the banks of the Colorado, the men used tin cups and frying pans and found much more gold. They could not inspect the river banks further, as the Indians were now more numerous and much closer. On that same day they left the river and headed east.

On August 3 they had their first serious encounter with Indians, a band of Garroteros who shot arrows at them throughout the day, wounding a few animals, including Aubry's famous mare "Dolly." The next day the Indians began firing at sunrise and followed the party all day. Aubry was hit by two arrows, and one arrow pierced the collar of Dick Williams. Several Indians were killed and a few wounded. This action took place in or near what is now Aubrey Valley, near the Yavapai-Coconino counties boundary in Arizona.

The Indians followed for a few days, even attacking the camp on the night of August 7, but they showed "less resolution" the next day and finally disappeared. Averaging about fifteen miles for the next few days, the party found a valley with good grass, timber, and water on August 13. On that same day the party met Indian travelers from Fort Yuma who had papers of recommendation from the fort commandant. In his journal Aubry does not identify the Indians, but a review of his trip in the *Santa Fe Gazette* stated that this band, too, were Garroteros.[3]

The next day, probably a bit to the west and south of modern Flagstaff, they camped near a village of Garro-

---

[3] Issue of Sept. 17, 1853.

teros. Adair wrote that "before we had unpacked, our camp was filled with men, women, and children   .   .   . all were on foot. They seemed quite friendly."

The extreme friendliness of the Indians made Aubry suspicious, so he selected a camp site on a small hill which would give him some fighting advantage. Adair estimated the Indian party as at least 250, and they practically fondled the travelers in an effort to show their friendship. In fact, "in our work we had to push them out of our way." [4]

When Aubry's party was saddled and ready to leave, the Garrotero chief took Aubry's right hand in a farewell gesture – but he retained his grip on Aubry. This was the signal to attack, and about fifty Indians, accompanied by their women, children, and babies, charged the party, using clubs and rocks.

This charge was the signal for phase two of the battle, as an additional two hundred Indians, concealed behind brush and hills, joined the struggle, using clubs and bows and arrows.

The plan of the Garroteros was to have several Indians hold each man while others clubbed him to death. William Baskerville, for example, was held so tightly that he couldn't move, but a Mexican managed to shoot

[4] *Appleton City Journal,* May 15, 1902. There is some confusion about Aubry's exact route. He normally entered in his journal the miles traveled each day, plus the direction. In miles he was not exact, but we do know that he used a compass. The best guess is that he followed his plan as well as he could – along the 35th Parallel. At the end of his journey he wrote: "I am satisfied that a railroad may be run almost mathematically from Zuni to the Colorado." Lt. Amiel Whipple in the same year traveled almost the same route, going from east to west (*Pacific Railroad Reports,* IV, pp. 7-9). E. F. Beale a few years later used Aubry's notes and wrote that he, Aubry, and Whipple traveled the same country, yet not precisely the same exact line; Lewis B. Lesley (ed.), *Uncle Sam's Camels,* p. 142.

every Indian holding him. As each of the travelers was freed, he drew his weapon and fired on the Indians. Aubry gives full credit to the Colt revolvers: "We shot them down so fast that we soon produced confusion among them." He praised the Colts as the "best that were ever invented." Francisco Guzman of New Mexico, and a Mr. Hendrey were particularly effective with these revolvers. The weapons were most likely Colt Navys, caliber .36 (often called Colt Belt Pistols).[5]

Tully, in his reminiscences, claimed that in the initial attack every one of the Aubry party was struck down except a Mexican boy and a German (Hendrey?). These two drew Colts and startled the Indians with their rapid fire, allowing others in the Aubry party to work with their guns.[6]

Adair didn't see much action. At the time of the charge he was filling canteens at the stream. Several Garroteros had happily accompanied him, and when the attack began they cracked his skull with a club.

The rapid fire of the Colts dispersed the Indians, and in the panic which followed many women hurled their babies and children down a nearby deep brushy gully, perhaps hoping that some would be saved; Aubry thought that this act probably killed many infants.[7]

Blood was everywhere, but miraculously none of Aubry's party was killed. All but two of the group were wounded, twelve severely. Adair was near death for

[5] Aubry's love for his revolver was not justified; misfiring of his Colt would lead to his death.

[6] Tucson *Citizen*, May 10, 1873. One journal article was particularly useful in unraveling of the Garrotero attack; Henry A. Bundschu, "Francis Xavier Aubry," *Pacific Historian*, v (Aug. 1961), 111-23.

[7] Both Aubry and Adair mention the throwing of the babies down the gully.

days because of his skull fracture, and Dick Williams, too, had a serious skull wound. Pinckney R. Tully, along for the pleasure trip, also had a severe head wound. Aubry himself was wounded in six places. The Garroteros were obviously skilled in the use of clubs.[8]

The Aubry party had been in great danger, according to Aubry the most perilous condition he had ever encountered. He also commented on the "trigger" for the attack: "On this occasion, which will be the last, I imprudently gave my right hand, in parting, to the Indian chief. The left must answer for leave-taking hereafter."

At least twenty-five Indians were killed, and many were wounded. Aubry reported that the captured and destroyed bows and arrows "would have more than filled a large wagon." These facts were in Aubry's printed journal, but he added an interesting point in his report to the new governor of New Mexico Territory, David Meriwether: some scalps were taken from dead Garroteros.[9]

The group patched itself up well enough to move five miles that afternoon, with the Indians still following and shooting arrows at them from a distance. That night moans and cries from the Indians lasted for hours. Adair called it "an incessant moaning and groaning and horrible howling."

The party traveled twenty miles in the next two days, still stalked by the Indians who continued to shoot

---

[8] *Santa Fe Weekly Gazette,* Sept. 17, 1853.

[9] Letter dated Sept. 30, 1853, in Letters Received, Office of Indian Affairs, New Mexico Superintendency, 1849-1853, Nat. Arch., Microcopy 234, Roll 546, frame 0638. Aubry gift-wrapped a scalp for editor Collins of the *Gazette* who commented that the chap who wore that "certainly waked up the wrong passenger" when he aroused Aubry; issue of Sept. 17, 1853.

arrows at them. Finally the Indians disappeared on August 17, the third day after the fanatical attack.[10]

The identity of the "Garroteros" has never been satisfactorily explained. The name *garrotero* is from the Spanish word for "club" and was originally applied to the Yuma proper, who lived farther south on the Colorado River. However, other "club" Indians, also of Yuman stock, in the vicinity of the attack were the Yavapai and Walapai. Some who have commented on the incident claimed the attackers were Coyotero Apaches, but we know from the rest of Aubry's journal that he could not have confused the Coyoteros with the Yuman Garroteros.

Furthermore, the type of surprise attack, the use of clubs, and the presence of women are all earmarks of Yuman warfare (Yuma, Mojave, Yavapai, etc.). Women were not stay-at-home types in the Colorado Basin, though the attack on the Aubry party was probably the most extreme development of this aspect of warfare in the Southwest. There is no evidence during this era of groups of Apaches wandering without horses and using women in an attack.[11]

---

[10] For further details of the Garrotero incident see Donald Chaput, "Babes in Arms," *Journal of Ariz. Hist.,* XIII (Autumn 1972), 197-204.

[11] According to Charles Smart, a surgeon at Ft. McDowell, Coyotero and Tonto were names for the same bands of Apaches; "Notes on the 'Tonto' Apaches," *Annual Report, Smithsonian Institution, 1867* (Wash: G.P.O., 1868), pp. 417-19. For Yuman warfare see A. L. Kroeber, *Handbook of the Indians of California* (Wash: G.P.O., 1925), p. 782, and Kroeber, "Yuman Tribes of the Lower Colorado," *Univ. of Calif. Pubns. in Archaeology and Ethnology,* XVI (1920), 475-85. In an otherwise sound work, Jack Forbes, *Warriors of the Colorado: The Yumas of the Quechan Nation and Their Neighbors* (Norman: Univ. of Okla. Press, 1964), p. 304, mentions once the "Garrotero Apaches" but makes no attempt to identify them. See also Kenneth M. Stewart, "Mohave Warfare," *Southwestern Jour. of Anthropology,* III (Autumn 1947), 257-78.

The fight had weakened the entire party. Most were wounded several times, the mules were giving out, and canteens and other equipment had been broken; they could carry water enough for only half a day. Their only food was half rations of horse meat, and Aubry was forced to eat the flesh of "Dolly," who so often, "by her speed, saved me from death at the hands of Indians." Dolly, too, had become famous in the West. In San Francisco, he had been offered $800 for the mare.[12]

By August 25, the men were eating berries and herbs, as it was unsafe to kill the few remaining animals. The next day they met a band of Tonto Apaches "who would cheerfully have committed depredations upon us if they had obtained a chance."

On August 27, about ten days from Zuni, they met a band of Apaches, in what would be a widely discussed frontier incident:

> We obtained from them over fifteen hundred dollars' worth of gold for a few old articles of clothing. The Indians use gold bullets for their guns. They are of different sizes and each Indian has a pouch of them. We saw an Indian load his gun with one large and three small gold bullets to shoot a rabbit.

Aubry did not know if the Indians obtained the gold themselves, or if they plundered it from travelers in Sonora. The Indians did not care for the gold; in fact, they first suggested that Aubry give them lead for the gold. Aubry and his men decided that the Indians were not Tonto Apaches, "as they do not speak any Spanish." In his report to Governor Meriwether, Aubry described the gold bullets and mentioned the Indians, "whose name I could not find out."

The party traveled on and arrived at the Pueblo of

---

12 Dolly comment in *Sacramento Union,* Dec. 6, 1853.

Zuni on September 6, where they were well received, and stocked up on provisions. The journey had been rough, but not a man had been lost, in spite of Indian attacks, severe hot weather, and near starvation. On September 10, Aubry reached Albuquerque, and he was in Santa Fe four days later.

On page one of the *Santa Fe Gazette* of September 24, 1853, editor James Collins, a longtime Aubry friend, printed correspondence he had exchanged with Aubry regarding the trip from California:

> Dear Sir: I congratulate you on your safe arrival in New Mexico, after a long and dangerous journey through a region of country hitherto unexplored, but at this time regarded by the public with intense interest, on account of the supposed existence through it of a comparitively faultless route for a railroad to connect the valley of the Mississippi with the Pacific ocean. May I ask you to gratify my curiosity, and that of the public, by allowing me to inspect your journals, and to publish such parts of it as may serve to give a full and correct idea of the country?
> Your friend, faithfully, J. L. COLLINS

Aubry had replied immediately, granting permission, and the journal, the Collins letter, and a flattering editorial appeared on September 24. Collins, in the editorial, reminded the public of the significance of Aubry's expedition – it could mean that the railroad to the Pacific would go through New Mexico. Although Aubry had not been on an official exploring party, Collins did not feel that this altered the importance of the Aubry journal:

> To those who know Mr. Aubry it would be superfluous for us to say a word in behalf of his veracity and good judgement. His friends all know him to be a man absolutely without parallel in physical qualities, and unsurpassed in all the traits of human character.

The Aubry journal as published was a daily account since leaving Tejon Pass on July 11. He finished his journal by making statements about the proposed railroad route. The Albuquerque Route (35th Parallel) was superior to the Gila Route (32nd Parallel) because it was more central and thus more serviceable to the nation. Yet it was far enough south to be free of extreme winter storms. The mountains were always in view, yet a route had been found through them. Aubry considered nearby mountains an advantage: they would furnish timber and constant streams of water, not to be found on the Gila Route. A few detours would be needed, but Aubry's conclusion was that the 35th Parallel, roughly from Tejon Pass to Albuquerque, would be ideal for the proposed Pacific railroad.

The Indian attacks had been frequent and strong, but Aubry believed that this in no way should figure in the selection of the route. Terrain, climate, and available fuel and water were the important considerations.

The Aubry journal was copied from the Santa Fe paper by newspapers in Saint Louis, Los Angeles, San Francisco, and his conclusions were widely publicized.[13] Although the railroad route was the major concern, some who read Aubry's account were more intrigued with the story of the gold bullets. The philosophy was stated by the *Daily Missouri Republican:*

He has, it would seem, seen hard and exciting times, and the idea of being shot by golden bullets strikes us as something decidedly new in the money-loving age of ours. Gold, it may be presumed,

---

[13] *Daily Missouri Republican,* Oct. 18, 1853; *Sacramento Union,* Dec. 6, 1853; *Los Angeles Star,* Dec. 31, 1853, are a few which contain journal extracts and Aubry's recommendation for a route.

is more plenty than lead, but it will not be so long if the Americans once get in there. We know how to make better use of it.[14]

Gold, railroad routes, and sheep trading were only some of Aubry's concerns during the trip. Aside from the notes he kept in his journal, he made other mental notes of interesting occurrences. In a discussion with ex-Governor Lane after his return, he reported black locust trees and sycamores between the Colorado and Zuni, as well as slate and other indications of stone-coal.[15]

Governor Lane, a week later, left by stage for Missouri, and in one of the more unusual aspects of plains travel acted as a courier for Aubry. He carried about $500 worth of gold, which was deposited with Aubry's banking firm in Saint Louis, Glasgow & Brothers.[16] Lane's brief tenure as governor came to an end because he had interfered in the work of the boundary commission. This nettled Washington officials, and Lane was replaced by David Meriwether. Aside from this incident, Lane had a fine reputation as New Mexico territorial governor.[17]

One of Aubry's strongest boosters was United States Senator William McKendree Gwin of California, a powerful member of several Congressional committees. Gwin was pushing all kinds of legislation that would provide California with better communication with the East. He arranged for the survey of the Pacific

[14] Issue of Oct. 18, 1853.

[15] William G. B. Carson (ed.), "William Carr Lane, Diary," *New Mex. Hist. Rev.,* xxxix (Oct. 1964), 301.

[16] *Ibid.,* pp. 303-04, entry of Sept. 30, 1853.

[17] *Los Angeles Star,* June 4, 1853, outlines Gov. Lane's problems with boundary politics.

Coast, secured the U.S. Mint and Navy Yard for San Francisco, and obtained regular steamship service between San Francisco and the Far East. Gwin especially wanted stagecoach and railroad connections across the country, hopefully something which would favor San Francisco.

In December of 1853, Gwin made a lengthy Senate speech in which he read into the record Aubry's entire journal of the 35th Parallel trip, agreeing with Aubry on the feasibility of a railroad on that route. He also thanked Aubry for not only providing a copy of the journal but for forwarding to Washington a map of the route.[18]

---

[18] *Speeches of Mr. Gwin of California . . . Delivered in the Senate . . . December 12, 1853,* a thirteen-page pamphlet, copy in Huntington Library. For a brief, useful sketch of Gwin see *Lamb's Biographical Dictionary of the United States,* III, pp. 448-49.

❧XI❧

The Last Ride

Intellectual improvement and care of his family had always been important to Aubry, from the moment he left Quebec in 1843. Over the years he continued to send money to his widowed mother, now living in Trois-Rivières, between Montreal and Quebec. To ease her burden, and to help some of his younger brothers, Aubry sent for Auguste, Joseph, and André and arranged for them to live in Saint Louis.[1]

Unlike most plainsmen, and certainly unlike the majority of French Canadians on the frontier, Aubry was an avid reader, grabbing issues of any newspaper he came upon on the trail. He had developed another talent unusual in the West: he could read, speak, and write excellent French, Spanish, and English. This was also beneficial to business dealings when travelling in such varied parts as Missouri, Chihuahua, Sonora, New Mexico, and California.

For the academic year 1851-1852, Aubry was enrolled as a student in the Literary and Scientific Department of Saint Louis University, a Roman Catholic school

---

[1] Tassé, *Les Canadiens*, II, p. 226.

operated by the Jesuits. The school, founded in 1829, had a large library and a fine museum, and hundreds of teenage boys from Missouri, Illinois, Louisiana, New Mexico, and Canada attended the institution.

However, a review of Aubry's trail activities for that era suggests he could not have spent much time in school. Perhaps he made the effort in order to encourage his brothers. The three of them, in their mid to late teens, were enrolled in Saint Louis University from 1852 through 1855, with all expenses paid by their now famous brother. There were dozens of other French-speaking students, most of them from Louisiana, Illinois, and Missouri. A few were Laurant Chartrand, Louis Comeau, Francis Allain, Martial Boudreaux, and Augustus Verret. There were also many Spanish-speaking boys enrolled, most of them sons of Aubry's New Mexico merchant associates: Francisco and Nicolas Armijo, Genaro Besanez, and several Otero and Perea boys.[2]

Aubry had decided while in California that the trade, and the adventure, were there, not in New Mexico. He planned a return trip to California; on May 4, 1853, from San José, California, he wrote to his friend Manuel Alvarez in Santa Fe, asking that merchant to purchase several thousand sheep for him. Money was no object, as "I shall take money to New Mexico to pay for all the sheep I may wish to buy."[3]

This pre-planning meant that Aubry would spend

[2] Catalogues for these years, listing the home of the Aubrys as "Three Rivers, Canada," are in the Pius XII Memorial Library, St. Louis Univ.

[3] Cited in Bieber, *Exploring Southwestern Trails*, p. 56; the original letter has since been lost.

only a minimum of time in Santa Fe. Because others had seen that Aubry had been able to drive sheep across the desert to California, they now wished to join in the second expedition. Francisco Perea, Miguel Salazar, Judge Antonio José Otero, and José Francisco Chavez, all prominent in New Mexico affairs, decided to go along with their flocks. Assisting Aubry again were two of his most trusted lieutenants, William Baskerville and Dick Williams.[4] Aubry tried unsuccessfully to enlist young John Hough for the trip, but Hough had previous commitments. In his reminiscences Hough, a close associate of Kit Carson, wrote that Carson referred to Aubry as "the greatest mountain and plain explorer."[5]

The opportunity to convert sheep into gold still attracted many adventurers in New Mexico. Kit Carson convinced Lucien Maxwell, Henri Mercure, and John Barnavette of the great California demand for wool and meat, and in February of 1853, while Aubry was heading towards Los Angeles on his first trip, Carson and party set out with about twelve thousand sheep for Laramie, Wyoming, then headed west to Sacramento and San Francisco. He sold them to businessman Samuel Norris for $5.50 a head. Elias Brevoort, who had gone out earlier, joined the Carson party in Los Angeles for the return trip. He claimed that some of the animals died under the weight of the gold ($20 pieces).

[4] H. H. Allison, "Colonel Francisco Perea," *Old Santa Fe,* 1 (Oct. 1913), 210-22; for Baskerville and Williams, see *Daily Missouri Republican,* Nov. 4, 1854.

[5] John S. Hough, "Early Western Experiences," *Colorado Mag.,* xvii (May 1940), 101-12.

In 1852 Dick Wootton "& Co." also took sheep to California, going via the Salt Lake City route.[6]

Henry Cuniffe, another Aubry Santa Fe friend, made the sheep-to-California trip in June, accompanying José Salazar y Otero, Antonio José Luna, and Raphael Luna. They sold "a large lot of sheep" to a Mr. Coons, but had much difficulty collecting the money. Nevertheless, they came back to New Mexico in August with about $70,000 in coin and gold.[7]

Aubry differed from these and other traders in several ways. To them, California gold was the magnet. Aubry wanted the gold, he wanted to find a satisfactory railroad route, and on both legs of the journey he planned to deviate from known trails, in order to find short cuts, beat others to the market, and add more fame to the Aubry name.

When the party left Santa Fe on October 10, 1853, there were about fifty thousand sheep, about one-third of them belonging to Aubry, the rest to Otero, Chavez, Perea, and Salazar. Aubry was, of course, in charge of the expedition.

At Albuquerque they met Lieutenant Amiel W. Whipple, United States Army, who was in charge of the government survey for a railroad across the 35th Parallel. Although Aubry was keen on the route for a railroad, he cautioned Whipple against using the trail.

---

[6] For Carson see Item P-E-8, Elias Brevoort Papers, Bancroft Lby.; *Santa Fe Weekly Gazette,* July 9, 1853; *Daily Alta California,* Mar. 6, 1854. For Carson and gold, see "Santa Fe Trail," Brevoort Papers, Bancroft Lby. For Wooten see "Agreement: R. L. Wooten & Co.," June 26, 1852, in Turley Papers, Missouri Hist. Soc. Most of these expeditions are summarized in Towne and Wentworth, *Shepherd's Empire,* pp. 90-91, but not with great accuracy.

[7] Cuniffe's trip in *Santa Fe Weekly Gazette,* Aug. 13, 1853.

It could be that although Aubry felt this was a good railroad route, it was unsafe for a small exploring party; he had memories of the persistent Garroteros. Before Aubry left Whipple at Albuquerque, he presented him with a printed copy of his 1853 journal.[8]

Again, Aubry wanted to alter slightly the route of his previous trip to California. Traveling with him was Dr. Thomas Massie of New Mexico, who kept detailed notes of the new route and wrote letters to editors in Santa Fe and Saint Louis describing the trip.

From the Rio Mimbres to Tucson, the party followed a new trail, somewhat south southwest. They found good grass and enough water. They crossed the Rio Salinas and Rio San Pedro and also found "many never failing springs." There was no timber to speak of, not enough, wrote Massie, to build a one hundred yard railroad. Yet the region was flat, and a direct path to Tucson was possible. This was the ideal route for travelers going from New Mexico to California, much superior to the route which went farther south via Santa Cruz. Aubry estimated that his new course chopped off fifteen days and two hundred miles from the other used routes.

Tucson, yet a part of Mexico, interested the party little. American money did no good there, according to Massie, as the people had nothing to sell. From Tucson the party headed west towards Fort Yuma, over an "irreclaimable desert, uninhabited, and forever uninhabitable by civilized man."

Approaching Fort Yuma, near the Pima villages, the Aubry party just missed Kit Carson's group by a mile or so as they passed in the night; Carson was returning

---

8 Bieber, *Exploring Southwestern Trails,* p. 57.

from his California sheep expedition. Aubry's horse
was lame, the result of fending Indians off the flank of
his flock, but he thought that at least Massie would be
able to see Carson and get details of the road ahead.
Unfortunately, Massie did not make contact. Aubry did
receive friendly notes though from his friends Henri
Mercure and Elias Brevoort, both traveling with Carson.

On December 8 the Aubry group reached Fort
Yuma, on the Colorado River. Aubry at first thought
the animals could swim the river, but then decided to
ferry them across for a fee. The whole operation took
more than a week. By this time the group had decreased, as Judge Otero and his men with their sheep
had stopped temporarily in Pima country.[9]

The Aubry party reached Los Angeles on January
10, following his route of the previous year through the
Mormon settlements at San Bernardino. Dr. Massie
was interviewed by the *Los Angeles Star,* which was
interested in the new route via Tucson. Massie described the trip and disclosed why Judge Otero had
stayed behind : not wishing to pay the exhorbitant ferry
fee at Yuma Crossing, Otero had built his own boat,
sailed it down the Gila, and at Fort Yuma transported
his ten thousand sheep across the river, saving himself
$1,500.[10]

During the entire trip to Los Angeles, Aubry had
lost only three hundred to four hundred sheep, indeed
a feat considering that he had taken thousands of sheep

---

9 This leg of the journey is described in detail in letters by Massie in *Santa
Fe Weekly Gazette,* Apr. 8, 1854, and *Daily Missouri Republican,* Apr. 18,
1854. For the Carson-Aubry "near-meeting" see *Daily Missouri Republican,*
Jan. 21, 1854.   10 *Los Angeles Star,* Jan. 14, 1854.

LOS ANGELES IN THE 1850s
With a population of under three thousand, the City of the Angels was still predominantly Mexican in culture and composition, relatively unaffected by the hordes who arrived in California seeking gold.
From Pacific Railroad Reports

San Bernardino

Aubry sold some sheep and mules in the new Mormon settlement on his way to Los Angeles. The town was booming during this period, however it radically declined temporarily following 1857 when Brigham Young called the faithful back to Utah.

From Pacific Railroad Reports

across new trails through desert and mountains. The economy, though, had changed from his last trip. Dozens of traders had purchased sheep in New Mexico, making the prices there rise. And the destination of the sheep was California, making the supply there abundant, with an obvious decline in price. Most traders at this time in California were asking five dollars a head, but Aubry planned to ask seven dollars when he arrived in San Francisco.[11]

Massie apparently left the Aubry party and arrived in San Francisco in late January; the Aubry party arrived a few weeks later without incident. Massie wrote the former governor of New Mexico, William Carr Lane, who wanted to be kept informed of Aubry's western activities. Lane had once traveled as far as the Gila River, and he sought further details of that section of New Mexico. Massie gave details of the route — vegetation, types of Indians along the way, and commented on possibilities of wagon and rail routes. He included some telling comments on Aubry:

> To you, however, who know Aubrey's extraordinary moral and physical endowments, there is nothing strange in this. I must do him the simple justice to say, that during a journey of three months with him, under circumstances eminently calculated to unfold to view one's whole character, I saw nothing but what tended to increase my friendship for him.[12]

Aubry's profit, after he sold his sheep in San Francisco and Sacramento, was "fair" according to Dr.

---

[11] Massie letters from Los Angeles and San Francisco in the *Santa Fe Weekly Gazette*, May 6, 1854.

[12] The letter, dated Feb. 12 and more than a column long, appeared in the *Daily Missouri Republican*, Apr. 18, 1854. For other comments on progress of the Aubry party see *Sacramento Union*, Dec. 30, 1853, Jan. 27, 1854.

Massie. That the sheep boom was over was becoming clear at both ends of the trail. Kit Carson, who passed near Aubry's party on the Gila River, later made an observation that hinted of the end of the sheep bonanza: he met about one hundred thousand sheep on the trail being driven to California. Carson swung off the old trail and followed Aubry's new route back to Santa Fe, saving his group miles and time.[13]

Aubry arrived in San Francisco when the Pacific railroad was being widely discussed. By this time his published journal of the year before had been reprinted by California newspapers, and the *Sacramento Union* praised the survey and mentioned that Aubry had sent maps of the proposed route to two powerful figures in American politics, Senator William McKendree Gwin and ex-Senator Thomas Hart Benton. In late January of 1854, Dr. Massie mentioned that Aubry's 1853 journal "produced great excitement everywhere" in California.[14]

Aubry spent the next few months in several California cities, shearing and selling sheep, selling and trading some mules, and planning the return trip. Judith Baskerville in a summary of her father's career states that Aubry trusted William Baskerville "implicitly" and used him as second-in-command. This was certainly the case in California, as Aubry shifted from San José to Sacramento, yet maintaining his headquarters and gathering his crew in San Francisco. Baskerville was in charge of selling mules, buying a wagon, and

---

13 *Daily Missouri Republican,* Jan. 21, 1854; *Daily Alta California,* Mar. 6, 1854.

14 *Sacramento Union,* Dec. 6 & 30, 1854; Massie comment in *Santa Fe Weekly Gazette,* May 6, 1854.

making other business arrangements for Aubry. Baskerville sold some of the mules to an obscure army lieutenant, Ulysses S. Grant.[15]

Life in California was still not attractive enough for the Aubry party. They met former New Mexicans in Los Angeles and San Francisco who were anxious to return to Santa Fe. While in San Francisco, Dr. Massie discussed the situation with a Mr. Gary, a successful businessman. "Yet, after all, he says he would not give 5 years of New Mexican life for twenty in California." [16]

While in San Francisco in April, Aubry discussed the 35th Parallel route with many, including Professor Jules Marcou of Switzerland, geologist for the Whipple expedition. He presented Marcou with some interesting samples of marble limestone he had found on the banks of the Colorado Chiquito River. Marcou referred to Aubry as "the celebrated *voyageur*." By this time Marcou had also become a firm proponent of the 35th Parallel route, and wrote a strong endorsement in *Echo du Pacifique,* a French newspaper published in San Francisco. Marcou felt that only a few tunnels would be needed; another advantage was the scattered deposits of coal along the way.[17]

The preparations for the return trip were completed

---

[15] Aubry letters of instruction to Baskerville, Apr. 7, June 19, 1854, in Western Hist. Dept., Denver Pub. Lby. Also in the Baskerville Papers is a sketch, "William Baskerville," by Judith Barber Baskerville.

[16] Two Massie letters from Los Angeles and San Francisco, written in January, are in *Santa Fe Weekly Gazette,* May 6, 1854.

[17] Jules Marcou, *Geology of North America,* p. 24. Marcou's *Echo du Pacifique* article was reprinted in *Daily Alta California,* Apr. 19, 1854. Marcou was one of the world's foremost geologists, holding key positions in France, Switzerland, and the United States.

by mid-June of 1854, and Aubry wrote the following
to the editor of the *Daily Missouri Republican:*

> I shall leave for New Mexico in 10 or 12 days. . . . I take a
> wagon and a boat. My object in taking a wagon is to make a
> trail which can be travelled at once, and the boat will be of im-
> mense advantage in crossing the Colorado. I shall at no time be
> more than 50 miles from my trail of last year, and frequently
> follow it; will pass through Zuni, and strike the Del Norte at
> Albuquerque or Peralta. The party will consist of over 50 men,
> and hope we will have an opportunity of punishing the Indians
> we met last year.[18]

On July 1, Aubry left for San José, and five days
later set out for New Mexico with sixty men, eleven of
whom had come west with him. His "companions" for
the trip were Judge Otero, José Francisco Chavez, and
Francisco Perea, and his foremen were William Baskerville and Dick Williams.[19]

The group hit Cañon de las Uvas on July 22, then
struck through the Tejon Pass in modern Kern County.
This, Aubry felt, was the lowest pass in the Sierra
Nevada and was best suited for a railroad. They arrived at the Colorado River on July 30, a distance of
about three hundred miles, traveling only in daylight
hours. The country was barren, but was suitable for a
railroad. At the Colorado, at the same site he had been
the previous year, the boat was unloaded from the
wagon, and the crossing was made the following day,
taking only ten hours. Perea and Chavez handled the
boat. Once on the other side they found some gold, but
found hints of much more on an adjacent mountain.

---

[18] Issue of July 15, 1854, letter dated San Francisco, June 15.

[19] The Aubry journal appeared in the *Daily Missouri Republican*, Sept. 26,
1854. Other available editions are in Bieber, *Exploring Southwestern Trails*,
pp. 376-83, and Tassé, *Les Canadiens*, II, App.

There were a few incidents with Indians, but Aubry felt that the large size of his party kept them safe. Along the way they saw several abandoned Indian rancherias, even bows and arrows. "Our men regret not having an opportunity of bringing punishment upon them for the treatment they extended to us last year."

From the Colorado River eastward he stayed fairly close to the trail he had made the previous year, starting to the south of it, crossing over, then going a bit to the north. They reached Zuni on August 17, and without further incident arrived in Santa Fe on August 18, 1854.[20]

His conclusion was the same as last year: the 35th Parallel was the best route for a railroad, though he suggested a modification at the extreme western end, above Tejon Pass. Furthermore, Aubry stated that the road he had just traveled was ideal for a wagon road, implying that the terrain was not difficult. This time Aubry took care of scoffers: he brought his wagon all the way to Peralta, south of Albuquerque, a fact so unusual that the story was even carried by the *New York Daily Tribune*.[21] The *Daily Missouri Republican* reported this wagon stunt with a comment from Dr. Henry Connelly of Santa Fe that this was "irrefutable evidence" of the practicality of the 35th Parallel as a railroad route.[22]

---

[20] Bieber, *Exploring Southwestern Trails,* p. 58.

[21] Issue of Sept. 26, 1854.

[22] *Daily Missouri Republican,* Sept. 26, 1854, which includes a brief editorial introduction to the journal. See also Thomas E. Farish, *History of Arizona,* I, p. 353.

≈XII≈

Trail's End

Aubry's trail finding was the necessary ammunition needed by advocates of the 35th Parallel route. In the spring of 1854, Senator Gwin managed to get his committee to favor a bill which would create a railroad from the Mississippi River to the Pacific Ocean, to be completed within seven years.[1]

Later in the year Gwin and his family visited Los Angeles and toured the country out beyond San Bernardino as far as San Gorgonio Mountain, examining this portion of the route that Aubry had recommended. Because of Gwin's position in the Congress, it seemed as though the 35th Parallel would be the chosen route.[2]

Another important explorer in favor of the 35th Parallel route was Kit Carson. In a letter published in several Missouri newspapers, Carson came out strongly for Aubry's route, claiming that the Utah route, farther north, was too mountainous and subject to sudden, severe weather: "I have no faith in it." He agreed that the Albuquerque-Los Angeles route was over barren

---

[1] Summarized in *Los Angeles Star,* Apr. 22, 1854.
[2] *Southern Californian* (Los Angeles), Nov. 30, 1854.

country, but the other suggested route, the Gila or 32nd Parallel, "is impracticable."[3]

There were still others that needed convincing, including ex-Major Richard Hanson Weightman. He had been born in Maryland in 1818 and attended West Point in the late 1830s; one report maintains that he was expelled for slashing a cadet with a knife. When the Mexican War began, Weightman was a resident of Saint Louis, and he offered his services in May of 1846. Battery A of the Missouri Light Artillery elected him captain. This was an elite group, and in addition to their flashy uniforms all the men wore a stout leather belt with a large bowie knife, one of Weightman's favorite weapons.[4]

The battery eventually reached Santa Fe, but seems to have been in only one battle, that at Sacramento, Chihuahua, in the expedition led by Colonel Doniphan. Weightman was discharged in August of 1849, "a most gallant and capable officer."[5] He settled in Santa Fe, practiced law, and got into the middle of New Mexico's turbulent politics. In 1850 he was elected Senator of New Mexico in an unsuccessful attempt to get statehood for the territory. He was a member of Congress from the Territory of New Mexico in 1851-52.[6]

[3] Carson letter in *Santa Fe Weekly Gazette,* July 9, 1853, from *Weekly Missouri Democrat.*

[4] Francis B. Heitman, *Historical Register and Dictionary of the United States Army,* I, p. 1014. There are brief biographies in Ralph Emerson Twitchell, *The History of the Military Occupation of the Territory of New Mexico,* pp. 381-94, and William A. Keleher, *Turmoil in New Mexico, 1846-1868,* p. 124. Weightman served as army paymaster in 1848; *Santa Fe Republican,* Aug. 21, 1848.

[5] Heitman, *Historical Register,* I, p. 1014; William E. Connelley, *Doniphan's Expedition and the Conquest of New Mexico and California,* pp. 361, 430.   [6] Twitchell, *Military Occupation of New Mexico,* p. 383.

Weightman was a gentleman with a temper, and there are many accounts, some most likely exaggerated, of his proclivity for dueling. During the Mexican War he had a disagreement with Lieutenant Edmund Chouteau, who said he would like to challenge Weightman to a duel, but unfortunately his arm was still in a sling. Weightman supposedly replied, "Oh, that's all right, I'll hold my right hand behind me and we will shoot with our left hands." The challenge was dropped.[7]

In 1849 Weightman publicly accused Territorial Judge Joab Houghton of conflict of interest, ignorance of the law, and dozens of other irregularities. Judge Houghton demanded "the satisfaction due from one gentleman to another," and Weightman eagerly obliged, wishing to square with this "fountain of Justice." A duel was fought near Santa Fe on September 19, with pistols. At the command "Fire!" Weightman shot, narrowly missing Houghton's head. Houghton, meanwhile, was apparently slightly deaf and did not hear the command. According to Twitchell's account, "Weightman then lifted both his hands in the air and told Houghton to shoot." The seconds stopped the ludicrous affair, but Weightman never retracted his accusations.[8] Weightman was an aggressive man of principle, willing to ride the gentleman's code to the death.

In 1853 Weightman entered the newspaper field, buying a printing plant and setting up the *Amigo del*

---

[7] *Ibid.,* p. 391.

[8] *Ibid.,* p. 392. Many documents in the Weightman-Houghton feud are reprinted on pp. 165-91. Weightman and others tried to force Houghton to resign; Santa Fe Petition, July 24, 1849, in Ritch Coll., Huntington Lby., Box 7. The duel is mentioned in *Daily Missouri Republican,* Nov. 1, 1849.

Pais (Friend of the Country) in Albuquerque in September. Within a few months it was obvious that the paper was going nowhere, so Weightman decided to move the plant to Santa Fe. Colonel James Collins of the *Gazette,* bitterly anti-Weightman, did the expected thing and welcomed him to town by announcing that they were busy writing the obituary for the *Amigo.*[9]

The relationship between Weightman and Collins extended far beyond newspaper rivalry. Furthermore, Collins approved of every Aubry action, even more reason for disparaging Weightman. In an 1852 episode of the Weightman-Collins feud, the *Gazette* wrote that "Weightman has already received more notice than either his talent or his worth can claim." In a particularly vicious attack on Weightman in 1853, the *Gazette* ridiculed him for appointing himself "Major General Weightman" of the Militia of New Mexico. Weightman, wrote Collins, could be found on any street in Santa Fe with a manuscript stuffed in his pocket, ready "to read to such persons as had the patience to listen to his silly excuses for various legislative delinquincies." [10]

Although Aubry and Weightman favored different routes for the Pacific railroad, after Aubry's return from the 1853 trip he seems to have partially convinced Weightman that the Albuquerque route had possibilities. For example, in the *Amigo del Pais* in December of that year, an article appeared on the Pacific Railroad Survey, including a letter from Zuni (Lt. Whipple's party). The *Amigo* hoped that in the near future it could congratulate the citizens of Albuquerque on being selected for the route.[11]

---

9 *Santa Fe Weekly Gazette,* Aug. 20, Dec. 10, 1853.
10 *Ibid.,* Nov. 27, 1852, June 11, 1853.

Weightman had met Aubry on the return from the 1853 trip in Albuquerque and discussed the route. Aubry then gave Weightman a copy of his notes and told him to "make such use of them as he thought proper." Weightman printed the journal and praised Aubry for his "enterprise and Public Spirit, at his own expense." Naturally, Aubry felt that Weightman had been converted into an advocate of the 35th Parallel route.[12]

But the convert became an apostate. When Aubry was in California for his second trip, a friend sent him a copy of the *Amigo* in which Weightman, in an editorial, "took back the compliment paid Aubry in his first article" and suggested he had been deceived by Aubry. The newspaper caught up with Aubry while he was in the Sierra Nevadas and made him furious. He wrote to a friend in Missouri, explaining that Weightman had lied about him because he still favored the Gila route "and can not tolerate views in opposition to his own."[13]

What Aubry did not know was that Weightman started again to favor the southern 32nd Parallel route because of the changing political conditions along the United States-Mexican border. In 1853 Santa Ana was again president of Mexico, and Southerners in the United States Congress exerted pressure to carry on

[11] More than anything else, the documentation for this statement explains the need for such a railroad. It was a letter from Zuni of Nov. 25, 1853, that appeared in *Amigo del Pais*, which was then shipped out of New Orleans, and appeared in the *Daily Alta California* of March 23, 1854.

[12] I have not been able to locate copies of *Amigo del Pais*. This series of events is based on a letter from J. L. Collins to his wife, Sept. 10, 1854, in Ritch Coll., Huntington Lby., Box 12.

[13] *Ibid.;* the situation is similarly explained in an article in the *Daily Alta California,* Oct. 20, 1854.

negotiations with Mexico to cede what is now the southern section of Arizona; they knew that Santa Ana was desperate for some quick money.

In December of 1853, James Gadsden, United States Minister to Mexico, convinced Santa Ana that money would be provided for that strip of land, and the United States would worry about Apache border-crossing war parties later. The Mexican government agreed, and the deal, known as the Gadsden Treaty, was ratified in the spring of 1854. Once again, Weightman could back a southern route, and favor the South, but this time the entire route could be planned through United States-owned territory.[14]

Aubry, of course, knew very little of this, as he was practically cut off from news of the East. When the *Santa Fe Gazette* first announced the ratification of the treaty on June 24, Aubry had just left from California on his return trip. Weightman, in Santa Fe, followed the political developments by reading United States and Mexican accounts regularly.

The stage was set for a showdown between two of New Mexico's foremost figures. Both were well-known men who disagreed on the most important issues in the territory. Also, both men had records of tolerating no abuse of their reputations; both had engaged in duels when honor was at stake. The return trip from California must have seemed long for Aubry, as he awaited an encounter with Weightman:

> Mr. Aubrey, though of a peaceable disposition, was a man who could not rest quietly under unjust imputations, and it is there-

---

14 Summarized from Perrigo, *Texas and our Spanish Southwest*, pp. 189-90; Twitchell, *Leading Facts of New Mexican History*, II, pp. 311-12; John Myers Myers, *The Death of the Bravos*, pp. 311-16.

fore probable that he sought redress from Major Weightman upon his arrival in Santa Fe.[15]

Aubry arrived in Santa Fe on August 18, 1854, about two in the afternoon, and a half hour later went to the store-cantina of his friends Joseph and Henri Mercure, located midway on the block on the south side of the Plaza. There were five or six people in the store at the time. Aubry refreshed himself with a drink of water, then asked for a toddy, which Mercure gave him.[16]

Meanwhile, Weightman was sitting near the corner of the Plaza, so he remarked to some friends that he would go into the cantina to say hello to Aubry. He entered the store and shook hands with Aubry, who still had his drink in his left hand. Aubry offered Weightman a drink, but he declined, taking a seat on the counter a few feet away. For a few minutes they talked about Aubry's California trip, after which Aubry shifted the conversation to Weightman; he asked why Weightman had not left for the States, as some had reported. Weightman replied that circumstances had detained him in Santa Fe.

Aubry asked Weightman what happened to *Amigo del Pais,* which was no longer being published. Weightman said it died a natural death, that is, lack of subscribers. Aubry retorted that such a lying paper de-

---

[15] *Daily Alta California,* Oct. 20, 1854.

[16] News of Aubry's death flashed across the country, but early reports were confusing: *Daily Missouri Democrat,* Sept. 21, 26, 1854, and *Daily Missouri Republican,* Sept. 10, 11, 21, 1854. For what follows I have relied most on the case of the Territory *v.* Weightman, Sept. 20-21, 1854, in Records of the U.S. District Court, County of Santa Fe. A lengthy article about the trial, including much verbatim testimony, appeared in the *Daily Missouri Republican,* Oct. 28, 1854. See also Twitchell, *Leading Facts of New Mexican History,* II, pp. 305-09. Twitchell, though brief and a bit confusing, based his account on primary sources.

served to die. Naturally Weightman demanded an explanation. Aubry replied: "Last fall you asked me for information about my trip, which I gave you, and you afterwards abused me."

Weightman heatedly denied this, and Aubry slammed his fist down on the counter and repeated the accusation: "I say it is so!"

Moving quickly, Weightman got off the counter, took a tumbler of water and liquor in his right hand, pitched the contents in Aubry's face, stepped back a few paces, and put his hand on his belt. Aubry at once reached for his Colt Belt Pistol, a five-shooter he carried on his left side. As he pulled it out to cock it, the pistol prematurely discharged into the ceiling.[17]

Meanwhile Weightman, seeing Aubry go for his Colt, drew a bowie knife from his belt and the two gentlemen of the frontier clinched. At this point Henri Mercure jumped over the counter and grabbed Weightman, and Joseph Mercure took hold of Aubry. Then, said Henri, "I saw a knife in Weightman's hand covered with blood. I told him to let go, and he said that Aubry was hurt." Aubry then collapsed into the arms of bystander Henry Cuniffe, uttering only "Let me bleed!"

United States Army Surgeon David C. DeLeon was sent for and arrived at once. He inspected the wound, which was a two-inch horizontal slash below the navel.[18]

---

17 This was the pistol (Colt Navy, Model 1851) which had so impressed Aubry in the Garrotero incident of 1853.

18 DeLeon stated that the intestines protruded about two hand lengths; *Daily Missouri Republican,* Oct. 28, 1854. The knife Weightman used was supposedly obtained from Antonio Tapia, who used it against the Apaches; Edwin L. Sabin, *Kit Carson Days,* II, p. 668.

DeLeon rushed to his nearby office for medical instruments, but when he returned he realized that he would be of no help, as the internal bleeding was severe. Aubry died on the floor of the Mercure store about ten minutes after the stabbing.[19]

After Aubry's death Weightman went to his quarters, which he shared with W. S. Cunningham. He unbuckled his belt, handed it to Cunningham and asked Cunningham's father, Major Francis A. Cunningham, to go with him to turn himself in to the marshal. Just at that time the newly appointed United States Marshal, Charles Blumner, showed up and announced to Weightman that he was under arrest. Weightman replied that it was right, in fact he was just going to deliver himself to Judge J. J. Davenport. The following day Davenport, the committing magistrate, held a hearing and set a bond for $2,000.

Burial services were held for Aubry the following day in the Catholic church, the Paroquia, with probably the largest crowd ever on hand for such a ceremony in Santa Fe. It was an expensive funeral, the church costs alone being more than two hundred dollars. Aubry had died in the midst of some of his best friends, and was buried in the presence of most of the people of greater Santa Fe.[20]

---

[19] See also "Tragica Muerte de Francis Aubry," by Demetrio Pérez, in Read Coll., State Records Center, Santa Fe. This differs in some details from accounts of trial witnesses.

[20] Funeral expenses are in "Record of Wills . . . Estate of F. X. Aubry," Hayden Coll., Arizona Hist. Soc., Tucson. Unfortunately the one issue of the *Santa Fe Weekly Gazette* which would have carried more funeral details cannot be located. The *Gaceta Semanaria de Santa Fé*, Sept. 16, 1854, announced that many people were on hand for the funeral, "friends who deplored his death." [trans.]

The trial of the Territory *v.* Weightman was held on September 20-21, 1854, in the United States District Court in Santa Fe, with the Honorable Kirby Benedict presiding. Judge Davenport had just left for the states, and Benedict was to handle all courts in the Territory that autumn; court was held in the Palace of the Governors.[21] The top legal experts in the Territory were involved; W. W. H. Davis, acting as attorney general, and soon to be the editor of the *Santa Fe Gazette,* represented the Territory. Serving as attorney for Weightman were John S. Watts, former associate justice of the Territorial Court, and Spruce M. Baird, a power in New Mexico politics. Baird was not only a Weightman friend, he also had business connections with him. A few months prior, Baird had purchased the machinery of *Amigo del Pais* from Weightman.[22]

The Mercure brothers, Cuniffe, Marshal Blumner, Surgeon DeLeon, and Major Cunningham testified. Although there were some minor contradictions in the testimony, the major points were consistent: Aubry, responding to the liquor thrown in his face, pulled a pistol on Weightman, who had made no move to go for a weapon.

Weightman, of course, pleaded self-defense. In his charge to the jury, Judge Benedict carefully pointed out that if they felt Aubry had drawn a pistol "with intent to shoot and greatly injure the person of Weight-

---

[21] Ralph Emerson Twitchell, *Old Santa Fe,* pp. 346-49; "Kirby Benedict," *Old Santa Fe,* I (July, 1913), 55-56. See also *Santa Fe Weekly Gazette,* Sept. 2, 1854, for court assignments.

[22] For biographical details see Twitchell, *Leading Facts of New Mexican History,* II, pp. 283, 310, 314-15. For sale of *Amigo* to Baird, see Keleher, *Turmoil in New Mexico,* p. 503.

RICHARD HANSON WEIGHTMAN
Weightman had been an officer in the Mexican
War before settling in New Mexico. He was
active in journalism and politics prior to
his fight with Aubry. He met his death as
a Confederate hero in the Civil War.
From *Doniphan's Expedition*

PARISH CHURCH OF SANTA FE
Much of the population of Santa Fe gathered at the Parish Church
for the funeral service following Aubry's death.
From *Old Santa Fe*, I, 1913

PASS FOR THE STEAMER "AUBREY"
The steamer, like its namesake, was "calculated for speed." (*see* p. 174)
Courtesy, State Historical Society of Missouri

man," and if Weightman had no means of escaping "without taking the life of Aubrey," then the jury "will find the defendant not guilty."

The jury, consisting of twelve Mexican-Americans headed by Vicente Garcia, deliberated about an hour and found that Weightman was not guilty, as it was "an act in defense of his person."

The general feeling was that the court, and the jury, had been partisans of Aubry, but the facts favored Weightman's acquittal. The *Gazette* felt that the trial was open and impartial, and no challenges of jurors were made by either side.[23]

The nation's press announced Aubry's death with sorrow, and many added words of regret that such a fine gentleman as Weightman was responsible. The Saint Louis *Daily Missouri Republican* reported that "much censure is attached to each party by their respective friends. It is said that no one regrets it more than Weightman."[24] The *New York Times* devoted an entire column to the tragic affair: "All who are or have been on the Plains will hear of his untimely death with a feeling of deep sadness."[25] Other lengthy accounts of the duel appeared in such distant places as the *Lake Superior Journal* of Sault Ste. Marie, San Francisco *Daily Alta California,* and *Le Canadien* of Quebec, which mourned "the death of our illustrious compatriot."[26]

Weightman, too, had a good press. Max Greene, who knew both Aubry and Weightman, wrote in the *New York Times* of Weightman: "amiable wife, beautiful

---

[23] Issue of Sept. 30, 1854. [24] Issue of Sept. 21, 1854.
[25] Issue of Sept. 19, 1854. [26] Sept. 23, 1854; Oct. 20, 1854; Sept. 27, 1854.

children, and many friends – is talented, a scholar and
in his bearing a finished gentleman. But the ardent
Southern blood in his veins, and living in a land of
bowie knives, have made him quick to resent the shadow
of an affront." Greene used similar exotic prose for
Aubry, "a man of forecast and alacrity. . . No one
attempted competition with him. Danger could not
appal him, unexplored districts were to him as familiar
paths . . . the emasculate and cowardly grew daring in his companionship." [27] One writer, signed as "K"
in the *Daily Missouri Republican,* regretted Aubry's
death, but referred to Weightman as all that was gallant, persevering, brave, and chivalrous.[28]

The great commercial entrepot of the West was still
Saint Louis, and thousands of French Canadians there
had almost deified Aubry for his many exploits. The
news of his death was a severe shock, and the *Revue de
l'Ouest* tried to put Aubry's life in perspective:

> He has rendered great services to the American people in finding
> better routes across the continent, and his name will be associated
> in the geographical history of North America with those of Mar-
> quette, LaSalle, Lewis, Clarke, and Fremont. [trans.] [29]

Unhappily for the residents of Santa Fe, the violence
of the Aubry-Weightman encounter was not an isolated
case. A few months after the event the *Gazette* complained that everyone carried a revolver or a butcher
knife. Weapons were "as much the part of a man's cos-
tume as the coat that covers his back." The last sentence
in this pleading editorial was "When will this crying

---

[27] Sept. 19, 1854.   [28] Sept. 28, 1854.
[29] *Revue de l'Ouest* (St. Louis), Sept. 16, 1854.

evil be remedied?" Apparently not for awhile. Two months later a few more of New Mexico's finest, members of the House of Representatives, carried a debate too far. The Speaker of the House, Facundo Pino, descended from the chair of authority, walked up to Representative Ramirez, and repeatedly clubbed him with a cane, knocking him down. Ramirez, a fine son of New Mexico, reached in his pocket for the always-present pistol, but bystanders prevented further blood. In all, a Santa Fe disagreement could lead to serious consequences.[30]

Weightman, to his regret, was known thereafter as the man who killed Aubry.[31] He left for Missouri on October 1, a week after the trial, and drifted back to Saint Louis.[32] At the outbreak of the Civil War Weightman joined the Missouri State Guard, a Confederate organization, where he served as colonel of an infantry brigade. He was a hero at the Battle of Carthage on July 5, 1861, when the Union Army was forced to retreat.[33] Five days later, at the Battle of Wilson's Creek, Weightman, wounded three times, died on the field just as the Union forces withdrew. General Sterling Price, CSA, reported that "among those who fell . . .

---

[30] *Santa Fe Weekly Gazette,* Nov. 18, 1854, Jan. 6, 1855. The readily available Dr. DeLeon was called in to treat Ramirez.

[31] One account reported Weightman "always saw Aubry before him – saw him dying in defense of what he believed his rights and his honor, and that he regretted that he had not allowed Aubry to kill him;" Connelley, *Doniphan's Expedition,* p. 629. "Although acquitted of murder, he never slept well after that, often waking up during the night and seeing Aubrey's face before him;" F. Stanley, *Giant in Lilliput: Story of Donaciano Vigil,* p. 172.

[32] *Santa Fe Weekly Gazette,* Oct. 7, 1854, notice of Weightman's departure.

[33] Ward L. Schrantz, "The Battle of Carthage," *Missouri Hist. Rev.,* xxxi (Jan. 1937), 140-49.

none deserves a dearer place in memory of Missourians than Richard Hanson Weightman." [34]

Aubry's French Canadian biographer, Tassé, ended by praising "one of our compatriots who has made for us the most honor abroad." His disappearance from the scene at the age of thirty, in full vigor of manhood, was a great loss to North America. Tassé's final comment: "Posterity will ratify the judgement carried by an American paper, that history will associate the Aubry name with those of the most celebrated voyageurs of the continent." [35] Such was not to be.

---

[34] General Price's official report is quoted in Twitchell, *Military Occupation of New Mexico,* pp. 393-94.   [35] Tassé, *Les Canadiens,* II, p. 227.

❦XIII❦

Forgotten Glory

The news of Aubry's death traveled fast across the plains, but not as fast as the great plainsman would have carried it. The tragedy occurred on August 18, 1854, and word reached western Missouri within three weeks, possibly earlier. By this time Saint Louis had telegraph connections with Independence and Weston, so any such news would have been immediately passed along. The first notice in Saint Louis appeared in the *Daily Missouri Republican* of September 10, a telegraphic dispatch from Lexington based on letters brought in by the freighting firm of Russell, Waddell & Co.[1]

Young Joseph Aubry took the stage from Independence to Santa Fe on September 3. It is unlikely that he knew of his brother's death at the time, as the rumors did not circulate in Missouri until a week later. Young Aubry, then, learned of the death of his famous brother while en route to visit him. A judge, a minister, and an army officer accompanied Joseph Aubry on the Santa

---

[1] See also issue of Sept. 11, 1854, for additional early reports. The telegraph had been extended as far as Weston in 1851.

Fe-bound stage, as did Colonel James Collins, just returned from Washington, D.C.[2]

Collins must have been furious, and appalled, when he received the news. To him, Aubry was not only supreme plainsman and premier explorer, Aubry was ideal man. And the killer of Aubry was Collins' archenemy, Major Weightman. Some of the reasons for this antagonism have been mentioned earlier. In his *Gazette,* Collins could use a phrase like "putrid subject" in referring to a Weightman manuscript and feel that he was being kind.[3]

When Collins reached Santa Fe he immediately wrote to his wife Eliza in Missouri: "I suppose you have heard of the death of my friend Aubry, murdered by Weightman, never was a more absolute murder committed and yet the murderer has been acquitted."[4] It mattered not to Collins that Weightman had acted in self-defense, that his own paper, the *Gazette,* felt that the trial was fair. For Collins it was a topsy-turvy justice – the worst evil prevailed over the greatest good.

Collins, Joseph Aubry, and group arrived in Santa Fe on September 25, delayed along the way by a breakdown of the luggage wagon. They missed the Weightman trial, which was held on September 20-21.[5]

On August 24, a few days after Aubry's death, his friend Joseph Mercure was appointed administrator of the estate, and the following month Francisco Chavez was appointed co-administrator.[6] Mercure had known

---

[2] For details of the trip see *Santa Fe Weekly Gazette,* Sept. 30, 1854.

[3] *Ibid.,* Nov. 27, 1852, for typical anti-Weightman article.

[4] Collins to wife Eliza, Sept. 30, 1854, Ritch Coll., Box 12, Huntington Lby.

[5] For arrival see *Santa Fe Weekly Gazette,* Sept. 30, 1854.

Aubry since the mid-1840s, and Chavez had made the last California trip with Aubry. The first major expense from the estate was about $700 to enable Joseph Aubry to return to Saint Louis University, collect brothers August and André, and return to Quebec.[7] Because the three Aubry boys were minors and thus were not considered appropriate administrators of the estate, Mercure was appointed.

For the next few years Mercure and Chavez paid off Aubry's debts, and received $500 for their efforts. In 1859 Father Joseph Machebeuf of Santa Fe was appointed administrator of the estate, at the request of Mme. Aubry, who was living in Trois-Rivières, Quebec. There remained $17,200 in the estate, and the probate judge listed the old $2,229 debt still owed Aubry by Joseph Nangle, which had led to the 1849 duel; Judge Antonio Ortiz wrote that the "note at this time is uncollectable."[8]

What happened to the $17,200 is another link in the chain of bad luck for the Aubry family which was begun by the death of François-Xavier. Aubry's widowed mother, Magdeleine, was sent a few thousand dollars by Machebeuf, who then pressured her into making a loan of $10,000 to the church in Santa Fe. Magdeleine Aubry did this reluctantly. For the next few years she repeatedly tried to gain control of the

---

6 Administrator's notice for Mercure in *ibid.,* Sept. 2, 1854; for Chavez see issue of Oct. 28.

7 "Estate of F. X. Aubry," taken from files of the Santa Fe County Court House, copy in Aubry File, Hayden Coll., Arizona Hist. Soc.

8 Probate Judge Antonio Ortiz statement, "In the matter of the estate of Francis X. Aubry, deceased," filed Mar. 26, 1859, copy in Aubry File, Hayden Coll., Arizona Hist. Soc.

estate. Soon Bishop Lamy became involved, and he was just as slow as Machebeuf in returning the money; in fact, he proposed another loan.[9]

Throughout the early 1860s there was a vigorous correspondence between Santa Fe and Trois-Rivières, with Bishop Lamy and Father Machebeuf writing that they could really use another loan, and Madame Aubry pleading that she was desperate, still needed money for her eight sons, and so forth. There were misunderstandings about the interest, and the sums that were sent to Quebec were usually late, due to the slow communications caused by the Civil War. Glasgow & Brothers of Saint Louis, where Aubry had formerly banked, handled the transactions.

Aubry's French Canadian biographer, Tassé, claimed that Madame Aubry was so grateful for the way that Bishop Lamy handled the estate that she donated funds to help in the construction of a school, convent, and other church buildings in Santa Fe. Tassé was not familiar with the inside story, and perhaps by the 1870s neither were the Aubry brothers.[10] It was not until the late 1860s that the hard-earned frontier money of François-Xavier Aubry finally arrived in Quebec.

Almost everything had gone right for Aubry until he met Weightman in the Santa Fe cantina. He was an idol of the country, on the verge of convincing the nation that he had found the best route for a railroad to the Pacific. But fate dealt Aubry a strange hand, apparently blank cards.

---

[9] There are eighteen pieces of correspondence regarding these funds in Loose Documents, Archives of the Archdiocese of Santa Fe, microfilm in State Records Center, Santa Fe; most are letters from Mme. Aubry to Machebeuf and Lamy, pleading for the funds.

[10] Tassé, *Les Canadiens,* II, p, 227.

For the next few years, as the results of the government surveys came trickling in, there was still considerable talk of a railroad. In 1856 the Cincinnati *Railroad Record* reprinted Aubry's account of his 1853 Tejon Pass-Albuquerque trip, emphasizing the pine forests, traces of coal, and ideal topography. In Santa Fe, this publication seemed to state the obvious, as the route was favored by Aubry, "that traveler, than whom few men had more practical views."[11]

And, greatest of ironies, Weightman, who had killed Aubry over the question of a route, finally decided that Aubry was right after all. Weightman moved to Kansas, and in 1859 he was one of the founding directors of the Atchison, Topeka, and Santa Fe Railroad, which was destined after the Civil War to follow the Aubry route along the 35th Parallel.[12]

Many observers realized that a stagecoach route must precede a rail connection. By 1860 many things were happening, as the Butterfield Stage Route (a southern approach) was functioning, and the telegraph lines connecting East and West were under construction.

Before the telegraph lines were completed, though, there was a brief, exciting period when the Pony Express operated between Saint Joseph, Missouri, and Sacramento, California, in 1860-1861. Here, too, was something that Aubry had anticipated.

No historian has been able to verify who first thought of the Pony Express, or when. Some accounts report that Senator Gwin of California, riding cross-country

11 *Railroad Record* (Cincinnati), Mar. 25, 1856; *Santa Fe Gazette,* May 31, 1856.

12 Frank A. Root and William E. Connelley, *The Overland Stage to California,* p. 425; *History of the State of Kansas,* p. 243.

in 1854 with B. F. Ficklin (superintendent for Russell, Majors & Waddell), discussed faster mail service and talked at length of Aubry's record trip of 1848.[13] This may have happened – it should have. All horsemen and travelers were familiar with Aubry's feat, and it would be ridiculous to assume that others would not try to copy Aubry. The difference, though, is that what Aubry did alone would now be done by dozens of riders as part of a team.

The first solid history of the venture was William Visscher's *Pony Express* (1908), in which he claimed that Aubry was the inspiration for the system. Arthur Chapman in his *Pony Express* (1932) devoted ten pages to Aubry's fame as a rider.[14] But we can ignore the well-meaning accounts of this century and turn to the most reliable of the 1800s, that of Bible-carrying Alexander Majors of the freighting firm. Majors had been a freighter for decades, and in his reminiscences he devoted a chapter to the Pony Express. Majors relates how the Aubry system was so thoroughly planned and executed that it became the model for the Pony Express. Majors knew Aubry well, and they met again on the trail in 1848 during Aubry's famous ride.[15]

Most modern accounts of the Pony Express give full credit for the venture to William Russell, with little or no mention of Senator Gwin or Aubry. There is no doubt that in the firm of Russell, Majors & Waddell, Russell was the wheeler-dealer, ready to plunge, to expand. According to Majors, in 1859 Russell met with

13 Everett Dick, *Vanguards of the Frontier*, p. 288; Waddell F. Smith, *The Story of the Pony Express*, p. 6.

14 Visscher, *Pony Express*, pp. 38-39; Chapman, *Pony Express*, pp. 17-26.

15 Majors, *Seventy Years on the Frontier*, pp. 182-93, chapter entitled "The Pony Express and its Brave Riders."

Senator Gwin in Washington; as usual, Gwin was pushing for better mail service to the Pacific Coast. He knew Russell, Majors & Waddell had a daily stage from the Missouri River to Salt Lake City. Gwin urged Russell to start a Pony Express on the line to Salt Lake City, then extend it to Sacramento. Gwin held the carrot in front of ever-eager Russell: make the Pony Express work and Congress would subsidize the scheme.[16]

Senator Gwin, of course, had long been familiar with Aubry's deeds. Like everyone else, he had cheered the dash across the plains in 1848. And in 1853, Gwin had been so impressed with Aubry's pioneering of the 35th Parallel route that he read Aubry's diary into the record of the Senate.

William Russell is usually considered the founder of the Pony Express, with some justification. Yet California's Senator Gwin had as much or more to do with the origins of the Pony Express as Russell – in fact, Gwin pushed Russell into a massive investment. So, contrary to most accounts, the Pony Express was born when Senator Gwin convinced William Russell to invest in a shaky venture. They hoped that the scheme, patterned after Aubry's proven relay system, would convince the nation, and Congress, to subsidize the new mail service.[17]

---

[16] *Ibid.*

[17] See also LeRoy Hafen, *The Overland Mail*, pp. 167-70. There is a vast literature on the Pony Express, usually dealing with lists of riders, who was the first rider out of Saint Joseph, etc. The most popular work today is Raymond W. and Mary Lund Settle, *Saddles and Spurs: Saga of the Pony Express,* yet they mention Aubry only in passing, never saying why. The claim for Gwin is controversial; an important Gwin speech, in which he details his interest in mail and steamship service, is in a supplement to the *Los Angeles Star,* Sept. 8, 1860.

Another touch of glory associated with Aubry was the steamer *F. X. Aubrey,* built in Pittsburgh in 1853 for service on the Missouri River between Saint Louis and Saint Joseph. She was, like her namesake, "calculated for great speed," and for a few years was the fastest vessel on the river. She had "proudly bearing at the head of its flagstaff the gilt figure of a horseman riding at full speed." Aubry, by this time in the California trade, never saw the steamer. The *Aubrey* was damaged in 1856, repaired, and finally dismantled in Pittsburgh in 1860.[18]

In September of 1865, Fort Aubrey was established close to where the Aubry Cut-off began on the Arkansas River. The post, which was intended as a temporary measure to deal with Indian problems on the Santa Fe Trail, was established by Captain Adolph Whitman and the 48th Wisconsin Infantry Regiment. The site was about five miles upriver from where the Aubry route began and was about three hundred yards from the Arkansas River. The post was abandoned in April of 1866, after the Indian troubles had subsided.[19]

Towns in Missouri, Oklahoma, and Texas were named for Aubry, and Kendall, Kansas, was formerly called Aubrey. Along the 35th Parallel, a few of the lasting names are those of Aubrey Valley and Aubrey Cliffs; there was a town of Aubrey, Arizona (Mohave County), at the mouth of Bill Williams River, but the site is now covered by the waters of Lake Havasu.[20] The

18 For construction details see *Pittsburgh Dispatch,* Apr. 9, 1853; quote from J. Evarts Greene, *The Santa Fe Trade: Its Route and Character,* p. 18. See also *S & D Reflector* (Marietta, Ohio), x (Sept. 1973), 22; this is a monthly journal of riverboat history.

19 Robert W. Frazer, *Forts of the West,* pp. 51-52; Louise Barry, "Fort Aubrey," *Kansas Hist. Quar.,* xxxix (Summer 1973), 188-99.

Aubry Cut-off, or Aubry Trail, that short-cut avoiding the *Jornada del Muerto,* was used throughout the 1860s, but decreasingly so. By 1865 the trail, no longer the new pioneered route of the early 1850s, was referred to as "the old Aubrey crossing." The movement of the railroads west would mark all such trails for oblivion.[21]

Perhaps if Aubrey, Arizona, had not been drowned by Lake Havasu, and a great metropolis had evolved there, we might now be more aware of the man Aubry. But the town disappeared, the steamer *Aubrey* was dismantled, Fort Aubrey was abandoned, and the Pony Express expired. And, although a railroad soon spanned the country, a central route, not Aubry's chosen 35th Parallel route, was selected.

The gold reports that circulated after Aubry's 1853 trip from California were widely discussed, then and later. Even Major Weightman commented on the gold in *Amigo del Pais;* he claimed that it had been worked with quicksilver, hence, had been stolen from miners by the Indians. However, another traveler in the region, José Maria Robles, obtained gold from the Indians, "evidently picked up on the surface of the ground." And, of course, Aubry and party had sifted the sands along the Colorado River and found much gold. The Civil War interfered with much prospecting, though there was a brief boom at La Paz in western Arizona. In the last half of the century Aubry's gold reports, especially that of the Indians' using gold bullets, re-

---

[20] For Aubry place-name information see John and Lillian Theobald, *Arizona Territory Post Offices,* p. 84; Bieber, *Exploring Southwestern Trails,* p. 62; Margaret Long, *The Santa Fe Trail,* pp. 17-18.

[21] Many comments on the use of the Aubry Cut-off are in "Early Far West Notebook, VII," Pioneer Museum, Colorado Springs.

ceived considerable publicity in books and newspapers. Yet no one has satisfactorily explained why the Indians were using gold, and where they had obtained it.[22]

Because of Aubry's meager, or at least well-hidden, love life, historians and journalists have not been able to stretch anything into a reasonable tale. In 1916 a newspaper article appeared entitled "Picturesque Hero of the Santa Fe Trail Acts as First Aid to Cupid." This rousing tale had Aubry and a trail hand, Edwin Gray, riding hard through the winter night to rescue a damsel stranded on an ice flow in the Missouri River. Naturally, of all the women in Missouri, the lady happened to be Mary Edwards, who had previously jilted Gray and had been forced into an engagement with her evil guardian. After the rescue, Aubry supposedly acted as intermediary and patched up the broken romance. There is hardly an ingredient of nineteenth century melodrama missing from this touching tale, but it most likely never happened.[23]

One aspect of the Aubry-Weightman clash deserves some examination: was this typical frontier justice? Many have written of the Code of the West, usually related to events of the 1870s and 1880s in the cow towns of Kansas. Ramon Adams listed certain characteristics of men who followed the Code: courage,

---

[22] The *Amigo* article was reprinted in the *Daily Missouri Republican* Nov. 11, 1853. For the Robles finds, see *Los Angeles Star,* Jan. 14, 1854. For other Aubry-gold comments see *California Farmer,* Dec. 14, 1860; *Prescott Morning Courier,* Mar. 6, 1888; *Arizona Enterprise* (Prescott), May 15, 1878; J. Ross Browne, *Adventures in Apache Country,* p. 69.

[23] *Kansas City Post,* Feb. 20, 1916. This event supposedly started from the Harris House in Westport. John Harris did keep an inn there in 1851-54; Barry, *Beginning of the West,* pp. 994, 1207. I have not been able to trace Edwin Gray; there is no record of him being on the trail with Aubry, though it is possible.

SAN JOAQUIN DELTA COLLEGE

MEMO TO..Date................................

From..

(To return cross out your name and the word "From")

SUBJECT...

Book Review for Pacific Historian

By Dec. 8 — at the latest!
monday

200 — 500 words

(REPLY)

Date of Reply.., 19........ By..

PUT IT IN WRITING · · · Written messages save time, prevent annoying interruptions, and reduce errors.

François X. Aubry

Trader, Trailmaker and Voyageur in the Southwest

1846-1854

by

DONALD CHAPUT

Natural History Museum
Los Angeles

One volume, large octavo, 250 pages; with a portrait, 19 illustrations, five maps including a two-color folding route map; bibliography, appendices, and index. A limited edition, printed in large Caslon type on high quality paper, sturdily bound in red linen.   **$15.50**

(Postpaid on prepaid orders; Californians please add applicable sales tax)

O F THE LIFE OF F. X. AUBRY and his often fabulous experiences, author Chaput has with historical care, interestingly woven the details into this highly readable presentation. Aubry was no obscure petty trader on the frontier. From 1846 to 1854 he was the busiest, most effective merchant on the St. Louis-Santa Fe-Chihuahua-California routes. His caravans were usually large, and his speed and reliability in getting the goods to the right market ahead of others was well known throughout the country.

His mercantile reputation perhaps was exceeded only by his developing a talent for individual travel that has never been surpassed. His eight-hundred-mile trip on horseback from Santa Fe to Independence in five days is a record very likely to stand forever.

The routes followed by earlier travelers did not satisfy Aubry. He spent his money and valuable time locating short-cuts on the Santa Fe and Chihuahua trails. And when the United States government planned the surveys of the 1850s for routes for a railroad to the

Pacific, Aubry made two overland trips from San Francisco to Santa Fe as his personal endeavor. His route along the 35th Parallel was later followed by the Santa Fe Railroad.

A few historians have mentioned Aubry and some of his achievements, but they have entirely missed the man. Aubry enjoyed, in fact cultivated, national acclaim. Honesty, bravery, reliability and integrity – these and similar attributes were consistently assigned to Aubry by all who knew him. His life was cut short by an early and untimely death from a knife-stab wound in Santa Fe.

Donald Chaput, the author, is senior curator of history in the Natural History Museum at Los Angeles. His research on Aubry has been thorough, though records are elusive. He has gleaned from many sources among which were contemporary accounts in widely-scattered newspapers, Aubry's brief journals, various archives including the Huntington Library, the Records Center in Santa Fe, the Denver Public Library, and sources in Aubry's Province of Quebec birthplace. Chaput has written extensively on western exploration, mining, the fur trade, and military affairs. His work has appeared in *Journal of Arizona History, Western Historical Quarterly, Colorado Magazine, Canadian Historical Review,* among others.

THE ARTHUR H. CLARK CO., *Publishers*
Box 230   Glendale, California   91209

loyalty, honesty, and fair play. Furthermore, every quarrel was private, so it was best not to interfere. For those who followed the Code, wrote Adams, it was "a life free from sham and hypocrisy." [24]

Aubry, though, violated one of the articles of the code: never pull a gun on a man who does not wear one. However, Aubry and his backers would maintain that the insult of the liquor in the face demanded stern countermeasures. It would be difficult to brand Aubry's act in the heat of semi-blindness and anger as cowardly. After all, everyone else in Santa Fe carried a pistol, so most likely he felt Weightman was also armed with one.

The use of the bowie knife by Weightman did not lessen his stature as a man of the Code. The well-equipped gentleman frequently carried a bowie knife. For example, Senator Cassius Clay of Kentucky even wrote a work on how to fight with a bowie knife: the best method was to get a headlock on one's opponent with the left arm, then slash his jugular vein. If this were not possible, one should sink the knife to the hilt on a line with the navel. [25]

Aubry's misfiring can easily be explained by the liquor in his face, his anger, and his habit of wearing his Colt on his left side. A man intent on firing, in this era or later, usually had his pistol out and ready. There are few recorded instances where "Quick-drawing" was used. As Joseph Rosa has recently written, "getting a six-shooter into action at speed in the heat of battle was

[24] Ramon F. Adams, "The Cowman's Code of Ethics," *Westerner's Brand Book, Denver Posse, 1949,* pp. 149-64.

[25] For Senator Clay, see Philip D. Jordan, *Frontier Law and Order,* p. 158. For comments on the widespread use of bowie knives, see Harold L. Peterson, *American Knives: The First History and Collectors' Guide,* p. 29.

not a common accomplishment, even among the expert gunfighters." [26]

What happened, then, in the Mercure cantina in Santa Fe in 1854 was the confrontation between two honored gentlemen of the frontier. The Code forced a showdown, and the presence of others made it impossible to withdraw. Each man had his favorite weapon, and one man was killed.

Yet evil was not defeated, nor did good leap upon a horse and ride into the sunset. A hero was killed, by another hero. If Weightman had been killed, the same sense, if not degree, of sadness, would have followed. The blood-spattered floor in Santa Fe was the result of good men following a code of behavior that had helped each carve his reputation on the frontier. It is one of the ironies of frontier history that these two giants of the era, who dueled to protect their names, have been ignored by historians.

Even Aubry's contemporaries could not properly record his name, usually preferring "Aubrey" to Aubry. And those few memoirs and reminiscences which mention Aubry usually confuse the first name. He is often referred to as "Felix," probably because he signed his name F. X. Aubry. Others refer to him as "Francis," "Frank," and "L.X." In correspondence, banking, and in placing of advertisements, Aubry most commonly referred to himself as "F. X. Aubry." To no avail, as the steamer became *Aubrey,* and the fort became Aubrey.

A sound appraisal of Aubry is hazardous for a variety of reasons. He was killed at the age of thirty, and most of his personal and business papers disappeared in

---

[26] Joseph G. Rosa, *The Gunfighter: Man or Myth?*, p. 125.

the confusion which followed. Other frontier giants, such as Kit Carson, Alexander Majors, John Charles Frémont, William T. Sherman, lived for decades after their early western activities. They, and biographers and journalists, had time to emphasize and embellish the record. What Aubry did, for personal and for business reasons, was indeed remarkable. Because of his drive and quest for fame, it is not unreasonable to assume that had Aubry lived for another thirty years, he would have been exploring in Alaska, shipping goods to Hawaii and Japan, and writing travel narratives to editors in Mexico City and Bogota.

Those few who have studied or known Aubry sometimes compare him to Kit Carson: they lived in the same vicinity and even crossed paths for a few years. Yet Kit lived almost sixty years, and some of his reputation was exaggerated by Eastern writers in search of a Western hero. Even great admirers of Kit Carson acknowledge that his future was made the day he linked up with Frémont. Aubry affixed himself to no man; in fact, if a man were involved in an activity that interested Aubry, he tried to excel, not to accompany.

The most amazing feature of the Aubry story is the unanimity of those who comment on his character. Aside from the expected praise for his trading, riding, and exploring accomplishments, one is bombarded with compliments to his honesty, friendliness, and decency. In the gambling houses of Santa Fe, in the usually male-only company on the plains, and in the city streets of Saint Louis and San Francisco, most people fell sometimes. Not Aubry.

No hint of a scandal, unkind business advantage, or personal slight appears. He had several duels, killed many Indians, and was involved in some famous controversies. But the duels were brought on by others, the Indians attacked him, and in the controversies he felt that his reputation was at stake. General William Tecumseh Sherman knew Aubry, both in Missouri and later in California, and his appraisal seems to echo that of everyone else who had contact with Aubry: "One of the best samples of that bold race of men who had grown up on the Plains." [27]

But Aubry was not just the great plainsman. He was born and raised as a French Canadian, and any evaluation of his career must consider what this means.

Samuel de Champlain in the early 1600s decided to send out young Étienne Brulé to live among the Indians, hoping that knowledge of the language and customs would be of use in French empire plans. It was, as by 1622 Brulé penetrated as far as Lake Superior, reporting on metal and furs in the region. Jean Nicollet followed, and in the 1630s he wrote detailed accounts of the Indians on the shore of Lake Superior. Within a few decades men like Radisson and Grosselliers knew most of the Great Lakes as well as Hudson's Bay.

Before the end of the 1600s the French influence, though thinly spread, was felt throughout much of North America. Missionaries and soldiers followed the explorers and trappers. Father Marquette would examine the Mississippi, La Salle the Gulf of Mexico, Le Seuer modern Minnesota, and in the early 1700s French travelers were to know the Canadian Rockies. [28]

---

[27] *Memoirs of William T. Sherman,* I, pp. 89-90.

[28] These paragraphs, and some of the following, are based on a series of articles I wrote on explorers, soldiers, missionaries, and Indians for the *Dictionary of Canadian Biography* (Toronto: Univ. of Toronto Press, II, 1969; III, 1974).

The impact of these trips was tremendous on the French population in Quebec. Life there was more restrictive than in the English colonies to the south, largely due to the centralization of government and because of the power of the church. Yet there was an alternative to the farm: a life in the woods. The general term *voyageur* can embrace most of those Frenchmen who moved north and west. For many Quebec farmers, a normal life was to work in the fields in early spring, then join one of the hundreds of large and small fur companies going north and west, often more than a thousand miles. Many Frenchmen never returned, but preferred a life in French frontier settlements by the Great Lakes or on the Mississippi, or in Indian villages as far away as the Pacific Ocean.

Historians and sociologists have a dozen reasons why these sons of Quebec were attracted to the often harsh, crude life of the icy North, the deserts of the Southwest, the Rockies, or the barren Plains. In addition to these "attractions" there was also the "push" factor of a non-dynamic society with frequent periods of economic depression in Quebec. There were also, of course, the intangible factors, such as the wish for adventure, an Indian maiden in every village, and the freedom from most government and church controls. Whatever the truth might be, by the time the United States obtained the Southwest in the Mexican War, French Canadians could be found from Minnesota to Texas, from Missouri to California and Oregon.[29]

---

[29] The literature on the *voyageur* is vast. Some of the classic accounts are Grace Lee Nute, *The Voyageur* (St. Paul: Minnesota Hist. Soc., 1931); Harold A. Innis, *The Fur Trade in Canada* (New Haven: Yale Univ. Press, 1930); Lewis O. Saum, *The Fur Trader and the Indian* (Seattle: Univ. of Washington Press, 1965).

Certain stereotypes became accepted over the years, based as always to some degree on reality. From earliest times a fur trade rendezvous was an occasion for wenching, drinking, and brawling, although by the 1800s this aspect of the trade had changed. By mid-century, if a composite of a French Canadian mountain man could be assembled it might resemble this: he was part Indian, short, dark, bearded, illiterate, always singing, had several female "alliances," fathered numerous children, was good on the trail, knew two or three Indian dialects, was a bit cowardly in direct confrontation, and knew most of the keys to survival. To see the partial validity of these characteristics one can read of the lives of some representative types: George Drouillard, Toussaint Charbonneau, Pierre Dorion, Jean-Baptiste Chaboillez, Joseph Rollette, Alexis Godey, Michel Falardeau, Julien Dubuque, Francois Deschamps, Louis Cadotte, Pierre Bottineau, and so forth.[30]

Aubry, as a French Canadian on the frontier, inherited but did not retain the normally assigned characteristics. Rather, everything positive in the stereotype was developed in Aubry to near perfection. He was the best trader, not a trader; he met death dozens of times before he fell; in horsemanship, no one could compete with him; he was friendly, hospitable, kind, considerate.

He had none of the negative aspects of the stereotype. He was more than literate, he was fluent and

---

[30] Dozens of biographies of French Canadians in the West can be found in Hafen, *The Mountain Men and the Fur Trade;* Morice, *Dictionnaire Historique des Canadiens de l'Ouest;* Tassé, *Les Canadiens de l'Ouest;* and in most of the state historical journals.

articulate in written and spoken French, English, and Spanish. He drank, but never to excess, and there is no evidence of any womanizing. He was more than a good son, as he provided for his mother and the entire Aubry family, even arranging for three of his brothers to attend Saint Louis University.

He apparently did have a volatile temper, evidenced in his encounters with Nangle, Pope, and Weightman. But in each of these cases it was a major cause that led to anger.

If a valid criticism could be leveled at Aubry, one might point to his attitude towards Indians. He never sought trouble, although on his second California trip he expressed an interest in revenge on the Garroteros. He never seems to have considered the Indians as having a right to the territory through which he was passing. If they attacked him, they were bandits, not Pawnees demonstrating that the land was theirs. But these are modern thoughts, held by few of Aubry's contemporaries. Measured by his times, he was neither an Indian lover nor an Indian hater.

Aubry was the *voyageur par excellence.* In the tradition of La Salle, Jolliett, and Radisson, he was an outstanding explorer. He added to this talent an aggressive business sense, interest in national affairs, and a horsemanship skill still unsurpassed. It is true that the desire for public acclaim shaped many of his decisions, but this is a human characteristic which should not be denied him.

⚜XIV⚜

Dramatis Personae

Aubry crossed trails with practically everyone in the West in the period 1846-1854. On many trips he was on variants of the Santa Fe Trail, Chihuahua Trail, and several different routes to and from California. His headquarters for these years had been Saint Louis and Santa Fe, two of the most significant centers in the West. What follows are a few comments about individuals who figured in the Aubry adventure in more than a passing way. For some, such as Frémont and Sherman, there is little need to add more here. For others, such as wagonmaster Dick Williams, the trail becomes blurred, and his later movements cannot be traced. Major Weightman's years after the death of Aubry have been covered sufficiently earlier in this work.

ADAIR, ABNER E. This young printer's apprentice witnessed Aubry's 1848 ride and in 1853 joined Aubry on the first California trip. On the return trip he was wounded in the encounter with the Garroteros. After recovering from his wound in Santa Fe, Adair returned to live in Missouri – for a long time. For decades after the Aubry "glory" years, Adair enjoyed reminiscing for the newspapers in western Missouri.[1]

ALVAREZ, MANUEL   He was a close associate of Aubry in Santa Fe and purchased sheep for the 1854 California trip. Born in Spain in 1794, Alvarez went to Mexico in 1818, and in the 1820s he entered the fur trade in the Rockies. From 1839 to 1846 he was the United States Consul in Santa Fe, an unusual position for one not a citizen of the United States. He was elected lieutenant governor in the abortive statehood try in 1850; in the following year he was appointed a brigadier general in the New Mexico militia. Alvarez made a visit to Spain in 1855 and died the following year in Santa Fe.[2]

BAIRD, SPRUCE M.   For one who at first disparaged New Mexican territorial ambitions, Baird made quite a mark in the territory. He was a Texan, sent to Santa Fe in 1848 to swing New Mexico into the Texan orbit. By 1851 Baird was a permanent resident of New Mexico and that year was elected to the territorial legislature from Bernalillo County. He defended Weightman in the Aubry death case. When the Civil War broke out, Baird's Texan leanings once more became open; his property was confiscated and he was arrested. After his release he joined the Confederate forces, serving as a major of battalion in 1863, and later as a colonel in the 4th Regiment, Arizona Brigade.[3]

---

[1] Some of these articles are in the *Odessa Democrat,* Feb. 23, 1917, and Sept. 5, 1919; *Appleton City Journal,* May 15, 1902.

[2] Harold H. Dunham, "Manuel Alvarez," in Hafen (ed.), *The Mountain Men and the Fur Trade,* I, pp. 181-97.

[3] Twitchell, *Leading Facts of New Mexican History,* II, p. 310, 398; Loomis Morton Gannaway, *Sectional Controversies,* pp. 22, 39-41, 62-64, 93.

BASKERVILLE, WILLIAM   He was born in Virginia in 1828 and moved to Missouri in 1837. He joined Aubry as a general hand in 1850 and was soon promoted to wagonmaster, a position he held until Aubry's death. Aubry considered Baskerville his most reliable employee. In 1855 Baskerville made another trip to California, this time in search of gold. He became ill there and followed a doctor's advice to change climate – he went to the West Indies and suffered for a few months. By the early 1860s Baskerville was back in Missouri, working as a farmer and merchant until his death at the turn of the century. His daughter claimed that Aubry's death was the last real event in Baskerville's life: "Curiously enough the remainder of his life was free from adventure."[4]

BEALE, EDWARD FITZGERALD   This adventurous "naval" frontiersman suffered with Aubry during the severe storm of 1848, and later, in 1857, Beale followed Aubry's route along the 35th Parallel while taking camels to California. Beale had served as a Navy lieutenant in the Mexican War; during the Civil War he was appointed Surveyor General of California by President Lincoln. Beale became known as the father of the California Indian reservation system; for years he owned the famous Tejon Ranch north of Los Angeles, the site which Aubry had recommended as ideal for a railroad route. Beale died in Washington, D.C., in 1893.[5]

---

[4] "Memoir of Judith Barber Baskerville," Western Hist. Dept., Denver Pub. Lby.; the Baskerville Papers also contain several Aubry-Baskerville letters.

[5] Lesley, *Uncle Sam's Camels,* p. 97; Conkling, *Butterfield Overland Mail,* pp. 109-10; *Daily Missouri Republican,* June 10, 1854; *Southern Californian* (Los Angeles), June 20, 1855.

BEALL, BENJAMIN L. "Old Ben Beall" took the field against the Apaches in 1848 to rescue Aubry's teams during the winter storm. Following this, Aubry and other Santa Fe merchants tried unsuccessfully to have Beall appointed governor of the territory. Beall was born in Washington (what would become the District of Columbia) and attended the Military Academy 1814-1818. He served as a captain in the Florida wars in the 1830s, and was a major of dragoons in the Mexican War, most of his service being in Mexico and New Mexico. He was decorated for gallantry at the Battle of Santa Cruz. At the outbreak of the Civil War he was a colonel, in charge of the District of Oregon. He was too old for active service though, retired in 1862, and died the following year.[6]

BENEDICT, KIRBY The presiding judge at Weightman's trial, Benedict had been appointed to the territorial court in 1853. He had previously practiced law in Illinois. Later, Benedict served for years as the Chief Justice of New Mexico Territory. However, his drinking and strange conduct, such as the use of powerful, vulgar language, led to his suspension from the practice of law in 1871.[7]

BLUMNER, CHARLES United States Marshal for the territory in 1854-1858, he arrested Weightman and kept him in protective custody until Weightman left Santa Fe. Blumner had been appointed territorial treasurer by General Kearny in 1846, a position he kept until

---

[6] Heitman, *Historical Register*, I, p. 202; *War of the Rebellion*, Ser. I, Vol. L, Pt. I, p. 675.

[7] *Santa Fe Weekly Gazette*, Sept. 2, 1854; Twitchell, "Kirby Benedict," *Old Santa Fe*, I (July 1913), 50-92; Hunt, *Kirby Benedict*.

1854. He served again as treasurer in 1857-1863, and from 1862 to 1869 he was the United States Collector of Internal Revenue in the territory.[8]

BREWERTON, GEORGE D.   Son of career general Henry Brewerton, George joined the 2nd New York Volunteers as a 2nd lieutenant in 1846, and the next year became a 1st lieutenant in the regular army. In 1848 he accompanied Kit Carson on a cross-country expedition from California to New Mexico. His meeting with Aubry on the trail in 1848 led to one of the best descriptions we have of Aubry. Brewerton resigned from the army in 1852, returned to the East, and for the next half century engaged in various printing and publishing enterprises. During the Civil War he wrote several military training manuals for recruits. His articles in *Harper's Monthly,* in which he described Aubry, were later printed in book form as *Overland with Kit Carson* (1930). He also wrote *Wars of the Western Border* (1859), dealing with the problems in Kansas. Brewerton died in 1901.[9]

BUCKNER, SIMON BOLIVAR   As commander of Fort Atkinson, Buckner met Aubry and became enthused about the Aubry Cut-off. Buckner was a graduate of West Point and served as a lieutenant in the Mexican War. In the early 1850s he was a captain serving at several western posts. Buckner resigned from the army in 1855 and returned to Kentucky to practice law. He entered Confederate service in 1861 as a brigadier gen-

[8] Lansing B. Bloom, "Historical Society Minutes, 1854-1863," *New Mexico Hist. Rev.,* XVIII (July 1943), 274; *Santa Fe Weekly Gazette,* Nov. 26, 1853.

[9] Heitman, *Historical Register,* I, p. 243; *Appleton's Cyclopaedia of American Biography,* I (1888), 370-71.

eral, and in 1864 he was promoted to lieutenant general, commander in the Trans-Mississippi Department. In the 1880s Buckner was elected governor of Kentucky, and in 1896 was vice-presidential candidate for the Gold Democrats.[10]

CHAVEZ (CHAVES), JOSE FRANCISCO Born in Bernalillo County, New Mexico, in 1833, José Francisco was a member of one of the territory's most prominent families. His grandfather, Francisco X. Chaves, had been governor of New Mexico, and his father was Mariana Chaves, chief of staff under Governor Manuel Armijo. In 1841 José Francisco was sent to school at Saint Louis University, after which he attended school for two years in New York at the College of Physicians and Surgeons. He returned to New Mexico in 1852 and met Aubry. He joined Aubry for the second California sheep-traveling expedition and was indispensible at the crossings of the Colorado River. In 1855 Chavez returned to California with sheep, but the market there was too depressed for much business. In the Civil War, Chavez worked to keep New Mexico in the Union; he joined the 1st New Mexico Infantry as a major and was later breveted a lieutenant colonel. He became a lawyer, was elected to several terms in the legislature, and in 1901 was appointed Superintendent of Public Instruction. His biographers claim that Chavez was the "foremost citizen in New Mexico of Spanish ancestry."[11]

10 Heitman, *Historical Register,* I, p. 259; Francis T. Miller (ed.), *Photographic History of the Civil War* (New York: Review of Reviews, 1912), X, p. 258.

11 Paul A. F. Walter, Frank W. Clancy, M. A. Otero, *Colonel José Francisco Chaves, 1833-1924,* a pamphlet; *Southern Californian* (Los Angeles), Jan. 25, 1855, Chavez sheep expedition.

COLLINS, JAMES L. This many-talented frontiersman was born in Missouri in 1801 and entered the trail trade in the West and Mexico in 1827. He bought the *Santa Fe Republican* in 1850, changed its name to *Gazette,* and from time to time served as its editor. He was Aubry's strongest champion, and most appropriately, Weightman's bitter enemy. He traveled across the plains with Aubry several times, and in the great debate over the 35th Parallel route, Collins backed Aubry exclusively. From 1857 to 1863 Collins served as Superintendent of Indian Affairs in New Mexico, and in 1866 became Receiver of the Land Office in Santa Fe. He was murdered in 1869 during a robbery.[12]

CONNELLY, HENRY Dr. Connelly attended medical school at Transylvania University in Kentucky, and in 1828 entered merchant life as a clerk in Chihuahua. Until the Mexican War he was a prominent merchant there; he settled permanently in Santa Fe in 1846. A few years later he married Dolores Perea, widow of the father of José Francisco Chavez. Connelly was an associate and admirer of Aubry and made several trips across the plains with him. In 1854, Connelly publicized the fact that Aubry's feat of taking a wagon from California to New Mexico was assurance that the route was ideal for a railroad. Dr. Connelly served as governor of New Mexico throughout the Civil War and was instrumental in keeping the territory in the Union. He died in Santa Fe in 1866.[13]

[12] *Santa Fe Weekly Gazette,* Nov. 27, 1852, Jan. 20, 1853; Barry, *Beginning of the West,* pp. 266, 916, 956, 1122, 1194; Bloom, *New Mex. Hist. Rev.,* XVIII (July 1943), 270.

[13] Twitchell, *Military Occupation of New Mexico,* pp. 365-66; *Daily Missouri Republican,* Sept. 26, 1854.

CUNIFFE, HENRY   This merchant came to New Mexico in 1846, served in the New Mexico Mounted Volunteers, and in 1848 opened a store in Santa Fe. He was a close friend of Aubry and the Mercure brothers, and he witnessed the Aubry-Weightman encounter. In the 1870s Cuniffe was probate judge in Mesilla; in 1884 was appointed commissioner of Doña Ana County.[14]

CUNNINGHAM, FRANCIS A.   Major Cunningham came to Santa Fe in 1847 and served as paymaster for the next few years. He was elected senator in the unsuccessful statehood attempt of 1850. His duties as paymaster took him many times on the trail, which he frequently traveled with Aubry. He was one of the few people in Santa Fe who was friendly with both Aubry and Weightman; his son roomed with Weightman. He retired in 1863 and died the following year.[15]

DAVIS, WILLIAM WATTS HART   Davis joined a Massachusetts volunteer infantry regiment in 1846 and by the end of the year was a lieutenant. He was promoted to captain in 1848, a few months before being mustered out. Davis arrived in New Mexico in 1853 to serve as the territorial attorney. His first major case as prosecutor was in Territory *v.* Weightman. Davis took over as editor of the *Santa Fe Gazette* in December of 1853, though Collins still owned the paper. For the next three years Davis was territorial attorney, editor, and for almost a year, acting governor. In 1856 he published *El Gringo, or New Mexico and Her People,* a classic in

---

14 *Daily Missouri Republican,* May 11, 1847; *El Republicano,* July 6, 1848; *Santa Fe Republican,* Jan. 22, 1848; "New Mexico Miscellany," Bancroft Library, item P-E7.

15 Heitman, *Historical Register,* I, p. 345; Barry, *Beginning of the West,* pp. 986, 1135, 999; *Daily Missouri Republican,* Aug. 18, 1850.

description, but loaded with typical Anglo-Saxon judgements about the inhabitants of New Mexico. Davis returned to live in Bucks County, Pennsylvania, but at the beginning of the Civil War went back to the army as captain in the Pennsylvania volunteer infantry (25th Regiment). By the end of the war he was a colonel and was breveted brigadier general for action during the Charleston, South Carolina campaign. Although Davis was fascinated with New Mexico, he chose not to live there. In 1883 he visited Santa Fe, where he was referred to as the "famous author and attorney." For years he edited the Doylestown *Democrat* (Pennsylvania); he died in 1910. [16]

DeLeon, David Camden   This native of South Carolina was the son of a surgeon, and he, too, became a surgeon in 1838, joining the army at that time. He was in most major battles in the Mexican War, and in the early 1850s he maintained his office at Fort Marcy. He attended Aubry but could do nothing to care for the massive wound from the bowie knife. At the outbreak of the Civil War, DeLeon joined the Confederate forces, with whom he served throughout the war. He later returned to practice in Santa Fe and died there on September 2, 1872. One source maintains that if DeLeon had not joined the Confederacy, he would have become the Surgeon General of the Armies of the United States. [17]

---

[16] Twitchell, *Leading Facts of New Mexican History,* II, pp. 314-15; Heitman, *Historical Register,* I, p. 361; *New Mex. Rev.,* Aug. 20, 1883; *Santa Fe Weekly Gazette,* Dec. 24, 1853, Feb. 16, 1856, discussing Davis' role as editor.

[17] Heitman, *Historical Register,* I, p. 366; DeLeon Coll., South Carolina Dept. of Archives and History; Harry E. Brown, *The Medical Department of the United States Army from 1775 to 1873,* pp. 177-78, 181, 190-91, 288; *Santa Fe Daily New Mexican,* Sept. 3, 1872.

GWIN, WILLIAM MCKENDREE   The career of this flamboyant physician-politican took him from Kentucky to Mississippi, Louisiana, then to California, where he served as one of the state's first two senators (the other was Frémont). Gwin backed Aubry's preference for a railroad route and did much to publicize Aubry's contributions to geographical knowledge. Later, in the formation of the Pony Express, Gwin was a key figure, and the Aubry relay concept for horses was followed. At the outbreak of the Civil War Gwin's preference for things Southern led to his imprisonment for disloyalty, but he was released and went to France in 1863. There he became intrigued with Maximillian's new government in Mexico, and he drafted a detailed scheme for the colonization of Sonora, which never materialized. He returned to San Francisco for a few years, then to New York, where he died in 1885.[18]

LANE, WILLIAM CARR   Born in Pennsylvania in 1789 and educated as a surgeon, Lane spent years as a post surgeon in the Upper Mississippi Valley. He settled in Saint Louis in 1819 and became a prominent educator and physician. In mid-1852 he was appointed governor of New Mexico Territory, but political problems caused him to resign in 1853. During his brief period in New Mexico, Governor Lane became an intimate associate of Aubry and accepted as ultimate truth everything that Aubry told him of trail conditions, railroad possibilities, geography, and any other topic of interest on the frontier. Lane returned to Saint Louis, where he died in 1863. The *Dictionary of American*

---

[18] *Lamb's Biographical Dictionary of the U.S.,* III, pp. 448-49.

Biography refers to his as "a record as lustrous as that of any St. Louisan of the years before the Civil War." [19]

MACHEBEUF, J.P. This important frontier clergyman was born in France in 1812, ordained in 1836, and came to America a few years later. He served in various Ohio Catholic parishes until 1850. In the following year he came to New Mexico and served as vicar-general to Bishop Lamy. The Machebeuf machinations with the Aubry estate are not among the more glorious chapters in church history. He later became the first bishop of the Denver Diocese and died in Denver in 1889. [20]

MAJORS, ALEXANDER Majors was the son of a merchant who was early in the Rocky Mountain trade. Alexander entered business in western Missouri and was soon in the Santa Fe trade. In the 1850s he did most of the freighting in the West for the army. He knew Aubry well, and left the only eye-witness account of the famous 1848 ride across the plains. Majors was the protector of Christian virtue on the frontier, as he provided all his men with Bibles, swore them to abjure profanity, and made Sunday a day of rest, no matter where the caravan was. By the late 1850s he was a partner in Russell, Majors & Waddell, the most powerful freighting firm in the West. When the Pony Express was started in 1860 by this firm, Majors installed the famous Aubry relay system. Times were hard for Majors after the Civil War, and he moved to Salt Lake City where he

---

[19] Bieber, *New Mexico Historical Review,* III (1928), 179-85, a biographical sketch; *Dictionary of American Biography,* X (1933), 583-84.

[20] Aubry estate correspondence in Archives of the Archdiocese of Santa Fe, microfilm in State Records Center, Santa Fe; Twitchell, *Leading Facts of New Mexican History,* II, p. 341.

remained from 1869 to 1879. He died in Chicago in 1900. His *Seventy Years on the Frontier* is a leading autobiography of the nineteenth century West.[21]

MASSIE, THOMAS E.   Another of the many Southerners who settled in New Mexico, Massie was born in Virginia and enlisted as a surgeon of volunteers in 1847. He was discharged the following year and remained in Santa Fe, where he became a leading physician. In the early 1850s he was the private physician to Territorial Governor James Calhoun. Aubry and Massie were close friends, so when Aubry promised Massie a bit of adventure on the California trip the offer was quickly accepted. Massie kept a detailed journal of the trip to California, and at various points he wrote lengthy letters that were published in newspapers in Santa Fe and Saint Louis. Permeating these writings was intense loyalty, almost devotion, to Aubry, both as a leader of men and as a moving example of ideal man. Apparently Massie had had enough of the frontier, though, as in March of 1854 he boarded a ship in San Francisco and headed back to Virginia, taking the Nicaragua route.[22]

MERCURE, HENRI AND JOSEPH   These Quebec-born brothers are best considered as a team, as they acted that way for almost twenty years in the West. In the mid-1840s they opened a store on the Plaza in Santa Fe. They made many trips over the Santa Fe Trail, traveling with Aubry when they could. They did business

---

21 His career can be understood by using his *Seventy Years on the Frontier;* see also Barry, *Beginning of the West,* pp. 122, 352, 1025-26, 1178, 1200, 1206.

22 Heitman, *Historical Register,* I, p. 696. His journal kept during the California-Nicaragua-Virginia trip is in the Huntington Library.

with the army and with the Indians, as well as a heavy trade with the citizens of Santa Fe. Both Mercures took sheep to California; Henri made the trip with Kit Carson. The brothers were Aubry's closest friends; not only were they fellow merchants, but they also had the same expatriate ties. It was in the Mercure cantina that Aubry received his death blow. Joseph Mercure was named administrator of the Aubry estate. In the following years the brothers had modest success as merchants, and in the early 1860s Henri served as Indian agent to a band of Utes in the northern part of the territory. His appointment was from James Collins, another prominent Aubry supporter. In 1863 Joseph had a mental break-down: he assaulted an army lieutenant, and proclaimed himself President of New Mexico. Henri was forced by the citizens to escort his brother out of town. Joseph was sent back to Missouri but never made it; he became ill on the Santa Fe Trail and died at the Arkansas Crossing. Henri died in Tierra Amarilla, New Mexico, in 1872.[23]

NANGLE, JOSEPH   Apparently a native of Missouri, Nangle was in New Mexico in 1846 and soon joined the Mounted Volunteers as a private. He opened a store in Santa Fe in 1847 and became a moderately successful merchant. He also served as *Alcalde* (Justice of the Peace), and in the 1850s was Commissioner of Public Buildings. When he refused to repay a loan to Aubry

---

23 *Santa Fe Weekly Gazette,* Dec. 31, 1853; Steck Papers, Univ. of N.M., Albuquerque (Mercure business receipts, etc.); Barry, *Beginning of the West,* pp. 1005, 1195; *Annual Report, Commissioner of Indian Affairs,* in U.S., Senate Exec. Doc. 1, 37th Cong., 2d sess. (1862), p. 736, Mercure as Indian agent; J. Robert Jones, "The President in Santa Fe" [Mercure], *New Mex. Mag.,* XXIX (Jan. 1951), 17.

in 1849, Aubry drew a pistol on him. The debt was never repaid; this seems to have been typical of Nangle's behavior, as many prominent New Mexicans did not trust him. By March of 1860 Nangle had somehow convinced others that he should be referred to as Dr. Nangle, and he was elected to membership in the Historical Society of New Mexico.[24]

OTERO, ANTONIO JOSE   Judge Otero had been appointed to that position by General Kearny in 1846. He was of a prominent local family and married into another when he took as his wife Francisca Chavez. In 1854, when Otero learned that Aubry was again going with sheep to California, he asked to go along with his own sheep, under the overall leadership of Aubry. He also made the return trip with Aubry. Otero later was judge of the Third Circuit Court, which included the area south of Santa Fe and most of modern Arizona, and served on the Territorial Supreme Court. He died in Peralta in 1870.[25]

PEREA, JOSE FRANCISCO   Born in Bernalillo County in 1830, the grandson of Governor Francisco Chavez, Perea was therefore a cousin of José Francisco Chavez. After some local schooling in Santa Fe and Albuquerque, he attended Saint Louis University from 1843 to 1845. Then, with his father and Dr. Connelly he went on a business trip to Baltimore and Washington in 1847. He returned to New Mexico and entered business as a merchant. He knew Aubry well and accompanied him on his last California trip. During the Civil War,

---

[24] Ritch Coll., Huntington Lby., Boxes 6 & 10; *Santa Fe Weekly Gazette,* Nov. 13, Dec. 25, 1847; Bloom, *New Mex. Hist. Rev.,* XVIII (July 1943), 286-88.
[25] Twitchell, *Military Occupation of New Mexico,* pp. 361-63.

Perea was appointed a lieutenant colonel of volunteers by Governor Connelly. In the 1860s he served several terms in Congress, and in 1888 was elected to the Territorial Council, the upper house in New Mexico.[26]

POMPEY Aubry's Negro servant was seldom mentioned by Aubry, or by other travelers, but then, neither were the dozens of other wagon masters and caravan hands. Apparently from 1847 on, Aubry had a servant. The Baskerville memoir defines his role: "Pomp, a free Negro, followed with Aubry's carriage, hauling the bags of money, medicine and Captain Aubry's clothes." Lieutenant Brewerton in 1848 included a few comments but confused the man's name, calling him "black Juba," "black Jake," or "black boy." Pompey did the cooking, set the prairie "table," and poured the brandy for the chatting session.

Pompey was more than a caravan cook, as he was responsible for the most valuable possessions while Aubry was on the trail. To have survived the Garrotero attack and subsequent hardships suggests that Pompey was well-adjusted to the frontier. He was also an outstanding rider. In 1847, on a sprint from Santa Fe to Missouri, Aubry set out with five men. Pompey stayed on Aubry's heels as far as Council Grove, much farther than the other four plainsmen, who couldn't keep up the pace. There is no word of Pompey after 1854, as the entire Aubry crew split up and scattered throughout the West.[27]

26 W. H. H. Allison, "Colonel Francisco Perea," *Old Santa Fe,* I (Oct. 1913), 210-25.

27 Baskerville Memoir, Denver Pub. Lby.; Brewerton, *Harper's New Monthly Magazine,* xxv (1862), 447-66; Adair reminiscences in *Odessa Democrat,* July 14, 1916, Feb. 23, 1917; Barry, *Beginning of the West,* pp. 730-31.

POPE, JOHN   Pope was born in Kentucky, attended the
United States Military Academy, and joined the Topographical Engineers in 1842. During the Mexican War
he was decorated for bravery at several battles and was
breveted a captain. He served in several western posts
in the 1850s, and was stationed at Fort Union in 1851
when he was detailed to find a short cut on the Santa Fe
Trail. Happily for both Aubry and Pope, they did not
meet while they were both claiming rights of discovery
for the Aubry Cut-off. Pope became a brigadier general
in 1861, a major general the following year. Pope had
several major commands in the West after his Civil
War service; retired in 1886, and died in 1892.[28]

ST. VRAIN, CERAN   Born in Missouri in 1802 of
French, rather than French Canadian parents, St. Vrain
became a merchant in 1825 when he went to Taos. From
1831 to 1847 he and Charles Bent operated Bent's Fort
on the northern branch of the Santa Fe Trail. In the
Mexican War, St. Vrain was head of the New Mexico
Volunteer Company and performed many services during the Taos Revolt. He opened a store in Santa Fe in
1847, near the Mercures' place on the Plaza. He became friendly with Aubry and they spent much time
together during Aubry's many trips to Santa Fe. Aubry
and St. Vrain visited Frémont in Taos, at Kit Carson's
home, after Frémont's disastrous expedition of 1848. In
the mid-1850s St. Vrain was a lieutenant colonel of
volunteers in several campaigns against the Utes and
Apaches. He died at his home in Mora in 1870.[29]

---

[28] Heitman, *Historical Register,* I, p. 798.

[29] Bloom, *New Mex. Hist. Rev.,* XVIII (July 1943), 299; David Lavender,
Bent's Fort, passim.

SENECAL, P.A.   A native of Quebec, Sénécal was one of many French Canadian merchants scattered along the frontier. He arrived in New Mexico in 1845, and a few years later joined Aubry, serving as wagonmaster. He was with Aubry during the trip of the White family massacre, and left a detailed report of that event. After he left Aubry's employ, Sénécal made a few trips across the plains with him. Sénécal returned to Quebec in the 1860s, and in the 1870s provided Aubry's biographer, Joseph Tassé, with many particulars of Western life.[30]

SLOAN, ELIZA   This lady of the frontier lost two husbands, the first killed in action in the Mexican War, the second killed by Indians near Fort Snelling, Minnesota. The widow and her two children moved back and forth from Fort Leavenworth, Santa Fe, Kansas City, Fort Union, and other Western posts, finally settling in Colorado, where daughter Marian married an army officer. Eliza, Aubry's only "potential wife," never remarried; she died in Colorado in the 1880s.[31]

TULLEY, PINCKNEY R.   This young Santa Fe lawyer went along with Aubry on the first California trip, expecting a pleasure excursion. On the return trip he was badly mauled by several Garoterro clubs. Yet Tulley returned to that region, later called Arizona, and became one of its leading citizens. In 1867 he was a political power in Santa Fe, but by 1868 he was established in Tucson. In the 1870s he was in Pinckney,

---

30 Tassé, *Les Canadiens,* II, pp. 179, 203-07; Morice, *Dictionaire Historique,* pp. 278-79; Barry, *Beginning of the West,* pp. 526, 947, 1089.

31 The memoirs of Marian Sloan Russell are in several consecutive issues of *Colorado Mag.,* XX-XXI (1943-44).

Ochoa & DeLong, the largest freighting firm in Arizona, and in 1879, he was a founder and president of the Pima County Bank, largest in Tucson.[32]

WATTS, JOHN S.   One of Weightman's attorneys in the trial of 1854, Watts was from Indiana and became a territorial judge in New Mexico in 1851. He began the practice of law in Santa Fe in 1854, and in 1861 was a delegate to Congress. In 1868 he was appointed Chief Justice of New Mexico Territory. He returned to Indiana in 1875 and died there the following year.[33]

---

[32] Tucson *Citizen*, May 10, 1873; Elizabeth Albrecht, "Estevan Ochoa: Mexican-American Businessman," *Arizoniana*, IV (Summer 1963), 35-40; Ray Brandes, "Guide to the Historic Landmarks of Tucson," *Arizoniana*, III (Summer 1962), 27-38; *New Mexican*, July 13, 1867, Aug. 4, 1868.

[33] *Santa Fe Weekly Gazette*, Aug. 19, 1854; Twitchell, *Leading Facts of New Mexican History*, II, p. 283; Bloom, *New Mex. Hist. Review*, XVIII (July 1943), 273.

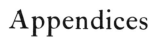

Appendices

Appendix I

CHRONOLOGY

1824 Dec. 3, Born near Maskinongé, Quebec
1843 To Saint Louis, Mo.
1846 May 9-June 23, Independence to Santa Fe (46 days)
       July 16-Aug. 17, Santa Fe to Missouri (33 days)
       Oct. ?, travel in Upper Mississippi Valley
1847 Apr. 30-July 10?, Missouri to Santa Fe (72 days?)
       July 28-Aug. 31, Santa Fe to Missouri (35 days)
       Sept. 25-Oct. 29, Missouri to Santa Fe (35 days)
1847 Dec. 22-1848, Jan. 5, Santa Fe to Missouri (15 days)
1848 Mar. 16-Apr. 21, Missouri to Santa Fe (37 days)
       May 19-May 28, Santa Fe to Missouri (10 days)
       July 15?-Aug. 5, Missouri to Santa Fe (22 days?)
       Sept. 12-Sept. 17, Santa Fe to Missouri (6 days)
       Oct. 8-Dec. 1, Missouri to Santa Fe (55 days)
1849 Feb. 15?, leaves Santa Fe for Texas and Chihuahua
       June 5, arrives in Santa Fe
       July 21-Aug. 23, Santa Fe to Missouri (34 days)
       Sept. 15-Oct. 30, Missouri to Santa Fe (46 days)
       Dec. 1, leaves Santa Fe for Texas and Chihuahua
1850 Feb. 1, leaves Victoria, Texas
       mid-May, arrives in Chihuahua
       June 11, arrives in Santa Fe
       June 12-July 3, Santa Fe to Missouri (20 days)
       July 10-mid-Aug., Missouri to Santa Fe
       Nov. 23, arrives in San Antonio, Texas

Dec. ?, in Chihuahua, then to Santa Fe
1851   Jan. ?, Santa Fe to Missouri
        Mar. 10-mid-Apr., Missouri to Santa Fe
        Apr. 23-May 12, Santa Fe to Missouri (20 days)
        June 29?-Aug. 30, Missouri to Santa Fe (63 days?)
        Sept. 19-Oct. 11, Santa Fe to Missouri (23 days)
        Oct. 23-mid-Dec., Missouri to Santa Fe
1851   Dec. 31-1852, Feb. 5, Santa Fe to Missouri (34 days)
1852   Mar. 1-Apr. 8?, Missouri to Santa Fe (39 days?)
        Apr. 11-May 8, Santa Fe to Missouri (28 days)
        May 25?-July 28?, Missouri to Santa Fe (65 days?)
        July 31-Aug. 25, Santa Fe to Missouri (26 days)
        Sept. 12-Nov. 5?, Missouri to Santa Fe (55 days?)
1852   Nov. 16-1853, late April, Santa Fe to San Francisco
1853   June 20-Sept. 14, San Francisco to Santa Fe (87 days)
        Oct. 10-1854, Jan. 10, Santa Fe to Los Angeles (93 days)
1854   Feb. 25?, arrives in San Francisco
        July 1-Aug. 18, San Francisco to Santa Fe (49 days)
        Aug. 18, killed by Major R. H. Weightman

Appendix II

CONTEMPORARY APPRAISALS

Aubry's reputation was based on his riding skills, his business sense, and his reliability. The following are a few excerpts from comments of his contemporaries, enough to give the flavor and degree of respect paid to Aubry by those who knew life in the West.

"One of Nature's most persevering children." *Santa Fe Republican,* Dec. 25, 1847.

"Such a rate of travel is unprecedented in Prairie life." *Daily Missouri Republican,* Jan. 11, 1848.

"We have every confidence in the dauntless zeal and indomitable enterprise of Mr. Aubry." St. Louis *Daily Reveille,* Mar. 19, 1848.

"His word is as good as the State Bank of Missouri." *Santa Fe Republican,* May 3, 1848.

"Such traveling is unexampled." *Daily Missouri Republican,* June 3, 1848.

"Extraordinary Traveling – Fourteen Days from Santa Fe to St. Louis." *New York Weekly Tribune,* June 27, 1848.

"The 'Telegraph,' as Mr. F. X. Aubry has been very appropriately styled." *Santa Fe Republican,* Aug. 9, 1848.

"Transcends the history of traveling." St. Louis *Daily Reveille,* Sept. 24, 1848.

"There is perhaps not one man in a million who could have lived to finish such a journey." Majors, *Seventy Years on the Frontier*.

"He seems . . . to have triumphed over all difficulties." *New York Daily Tribune*, Feb. 28, 1849.

"Mr. F. X. Aubry – this Gentleman travels with a rapidity almost super-natural." *Santa Fe Republican*, Aug. 9, 1849.

"The generous-hearted 'Telegraph,' Aubrey." *Daily Missouri Republican*, Dec. 19, 1849.

"The 'fastest man' on record, Mr. F. X. Aubrey." St. Louis *Daily Reveille*, July 9, 1850.

"Mr. Aubry, the great Plains Courier." *Daily Missouri Republican*, Feb. 2, 1852.

"Mr. F. X. Aubry, the justly distinguished Santa Fe trader." *Daily Missouri Republican*, Feb. 15, 1852.

"No season or weather stops him." *Daily Missouri Republican*, Feb. 16, 1852.

"Mr. F. X. Aubry, the fleet traveler of the Prairie." *Daily Missouri Republican*, Aug. 31, 1852.

"Capt. F. X. Aubry, whose name has become celebrated by his perilous trips in the mountains and deserts." *Sacramento Union*, Dec. 30, 1853.

"Our illustrious compatriot." Montreal *La Minerve*, Sept. 26, 1854.

"F. X. Aubrey, the most daring and enthusiastic traveller of the age." Los Angeles *Southern Californian*, Oct. 19, 1854.

Appendix III

THE AUBRY JOURNALS

Of the dozen or so published Aubry journals, the most important are the ones of the California-New Mexico trips, 1853 and 1854. Travelers, government officials, Indian agents, Army engineers, and railroad planners read them eagerly, as did prospectors. However, the journals are readily available, and it would serve little purpose to reprint them here. These journals first were printed in the *Santa Fe Gazette,* then picked up by other Midwestern and Western newspapers. They were later printed in such publications as the *Congressional Globe* and the *Railroad Record.* In more accessible form the journals can be found in Tassé, *Les Canadiens de l'Ouest,* Volume II, in Bieber, *Exploring Southwestern Trails,* and Wyman, *New Mexico Historical Review,* VII (1932).

An Aubry biography, though, does seem a logical place to include some of his shorter, earlier journals. He kept a journal on his first return trip from Santa Fe to Missouri in 1846, and generally took notes or kept a complete journal in the succeeding years. On some occasions he could not do so, as the need for trail speed did not allow him the opportunity. On another occasion, an 1852 trip through an unexplored region, Aubry kept notes, but they were not published. Instead, the *Daily Missouri Republican* printed the notes of New Mexico Territorial Secretary William S. Allen, who traveled with the party and obviously discussed the route – and the article – with Aubry.

The newspapers in Missouri published dozens of journals from travelers, because during and after the Mexican War thousands of soldiers from Missouri and nearby states were scattered along the Santa Fe Trail and further south and west. Movements of troops, and conditions along the trail, often provided only by such journals, were eagerly sought by editors for their readers. Even though towns like Westport, Independence, and Saint Joseph were the jump-off points, Saint Louis was the commercial entrepot on which they drew their equipment and supplies. Most of the printed Aubry journals appeared in Saint Louis newspapers.

The following Aubry journals are representative of those that he kept during the period 1846-1852. They are unadorned accounts of life and activity along one of North America's most vital transportation routes. The wording and spelling have not been altered.

1846 This journal appeared in the *Daily Missouri Republican* of August 24. The editor included one column of news under the title "Late from Santa Fe." He announced that Aubry and other travelers had reached Independence on August 17. In three paragraphs the editor summarized the news from New Mexico and Chihuahua, as relayed from Aubry, then included the following portion of Aubry's journal:

On the 3d of August, met twelve government wagons at Coon Creek; 6th, met forty-two government wagons at Ash Creek; 7th, met three traders wagons, bound for Taos, at Big Cow Creek, and twenty government wagons at Small Cow Creek; also, two belonging to traders, whose names were not known; 8th, met Magoffin's party at Turkey creek; 9th, met Armijo's wagons at Lost Spring; 10th, met 21 government wagons at Diamond Spring, and on the 11th, thirty more at Council Grove; on the same day, met twenty wagons belonging to Mexican traders, at Bean creek; 12th, met Algeuer with twenty wagons at Turtle creek; 13th, met six wagons belonging to traders, bound for the mountains in New Mexico; also, seven traders' wagons at creek No. 110. On the same day, met at Adam's grove the company of volunteers from Platte and Monroe counties; 14th, met the Boone county company at Hickory Point, and on the same day, met Gentry with forty-five wagons, at Black Jack.

1847 Aubry arrived in Independence on September 1, and the *Daily Missouri Republican* announced that fact and published his journal in the issue of September 6. Aside from his journal, Aubry also had much news from Chihuahua and other points in the West, and this was printed, followed by the editor's comment: "Mr. Aubry has kindly permitted me to extract the following from the memoranda, on the way in."

August 1st – Met at the Wagon Mound, a company of U.S. Dragoons, under charge of Lieut. Love, with a large sum of money for the payment of the troops, and a train of Government wagons, in care of Fagan, of Platte City. Messrs. Fitzpatrick, Wetherhead, Turley, Wally and Lieut. Dewitt, also accompanying them.

August 8th – At McKnees' Creek, met Col. Easton, of St. Louis, with the five companies of Missouri volunteers, under Captains Paul, Cunningham, Barnes, Shepherd, Weckner. They had in charge a train of Government wagons. The traders along were Messrs. Stevenson, Coons, McIntosh, Cuniffe, McGill,

Drack, Williams, Estis, Carr, Rohman, and Kearney, with forty wagons filled with dry goods and provisions.

August 10th – Met, at Cold Spring, a company of mounted Missouri volunteers, under charge of Capt. Jones, who had two pieces of artillery along. Emanuel Armijo is in company, with twenty wagons.

August 12th – Above Middle Spring, I saw Messrs. Murphy and Post, Wm. McKnight, Owens and Woops, with twenty wagons.

August 13th – At Middle Spring, met four companies of Missouri volunteers, Capts. Korponay, Boke, Clarkson, and Smithson; two trains government wagons – Thompson and Hayden, wagon masters. Messrs. Emerson, Turner, Allen and Teabout, of St. Louis, were along, with ten wagons. Next day, Simonds' company of volunteers, a little below the Spring, were met, protecting a government train – Coffman, of Platte, wagon master. Bailey, ..., of Clarkson's company, and W. B. Howell of Simonds company, died a little below the Middle Spring.

August 16 – met, at Sand Creek, Lofflin's Company of Missouri Mounted Volunteers, and a train of Gov't wagons. Lt. Col. Hovaken and three companies of Illinois Infantry, Capts. Hook, Cunningham, and Turner, and two trains of government wagons, in charge of Finley, of Westport.

18th – at Battle Ground, met Col. Newby, of Illinois, and three companies of Infantry. Reed, Moses and Kinney, Captains; also, Barclay, of Lexington Mo. and Thorp, of St. Louis, with seven wagons of goods and provisions.

19th – Ford of Arkansas, met Major Donaldson and Companies A, B, J, K Illinois Infantry, and Hontington's train of government wagons.

Aug. 28 – At Little Arkansas, met Col. Ralls, with two companies Missouri Mounted Volunteers; also Capts. McNair, Haley and Geis, as well as five trains government wagons, and Stone, Goldstein, and other traders.

August 29th – Met at Cotton Wood, Symington & Renning's train of Government Wagons. At Council Grove, St. Vrain's (DeLisle & Bauvais, of St. Louis) twenty wagons.

August 30th – At creek 142, Mr. St. Vrain and Barclay, with six wagons of provisions. At Soldiers' Creek, met Messrs. Noland, Harrison, Herrald and Oldham, of Independence, with twelve wagons of provisions. At Bridge Creek, Mr. Colter, and lady, of St. Louis, and Smith, of the firm of Colburn & Smith. At Willow Spring, Mr. Hays, Indian trader. At Hickory Point, Messrs. White & Simpson, Sutlers to Ralls' Regiment, and traders to Santa Fe.

1847-1848 On Aubry's last trip of 1847, he left Santa Fe on December 21 and arrived in Independence on January 5, 1848. This was one of his earliest quick trips, made in fourteen days. The following account appeared in the Saint Louis *Daily Reveille* of January 12, 1848. Aubry may have kept some travel notes which he referred to when questioned by the *Reveille* correspondent in Independence. The phrases used, though, indicate that the information was gathered primarily during an interview ("He states," "Mr. Aubrey represents," "I append the substance, as near I can gather from Mr. A.," etc.).

Eds. of the Reveille – GENTLEMEN : – Mr. F. X. Aubrey arrived in our town, this evening, direct from Santa Fe, making the quickest trip ever yet made across the plains – making the entire trip in fourteen days, including two which he lost on the route! He left Santa Fe on the 21st of last month, in company with four others, but came here alone, having left the balance of his company at the Cotton Wood. In the last three days he has travelled 306 miles! He states that Col. Price had reached Santa Fe before he left, and had made but little alteration in the disposition of the troops from that heretofore made by Col. Newby. He states that Gov. Armijo was recently captured by our troops at El Paso, but that he had violated his parole of honor, and *sloped* for *Chihuahua!* The Governor acted upon the old adage, which says that, "he that fights and runs away, may have to fight another day," etc. The Governor, it seems, was allowed to go at pleasure within the limits of the town of El Paso; but at the first opportunity he made his escape. He had made every effort with the people in and about El Paso, to raise a sufficient force to prevent our troops from entering that place, but they would not listen to this, although he offered large sums of money to induce a "turn out."

Mr. Aubrey represents everything in Santa Fe, as going on well, without any probability of disturbances of any kind. He states that a Government express started three days before he did, which, in all probability, will be at Fort Leavenworth in a few days. Mr. Aubrey says, he saw no Indians on the route, and had but four days of severe cold weather. He made "mule flesh" suffer, however, as he killed three, by hard travelling on the way.

I append the substance, as near I can gather from Mr. A., of what had transpired at Santa Fe previous to his departure.

The Legislature of New Mexico convened on the 6th of December. Capt. Angney, Speaker of the House; Antonio Sandival, President of the Senate; James Giddings, Clerk of Lower House; George K. Gibson, Enrolling Clerk; E. J. Vaughn, Door-keeper. Henry Henry was elected Clerk of the Senate; J. Hubble, Door-keeper, and Jose Abran, Enrolling Clerk.

Lieut. Gov. Donaciano Vigil has been promoted, by Gen. Price, to the chief Gubernatorial chair of New Mexico. His message to the Legislature is spoken of as a sensible document.

Ortiz, of Taos, offered a resolution in the Legislature, proposing to adjourn until next summer, which was negatived.

A bill was before the House, calling a convention to take into consideration the annexation of the territory of New Mexico to the United States. This bill provides, "1st. That an election shall be held in the several counties (fifteen days after this Legislature adjourns) for the election of delegates to take into consideration the annexation of this Territory to the United States; and in case it meets with approbation, to devise such measures and adopt such acts, as will most speedily effect the same."

Lieut. Paul, of the Missouri battalion, arrived at Santa Fe on the 10th, from Socorro.

The three battalions – Walker's, Illinois, and Missouri – are reported in good health.

1848 When Aubry made his record-breaking ride in this year he did not keep a journal, but he made mental notes of events along the trail. The *Daily Missouri Republican* praised Aubry in an article entitled "Most Extraordinary Trip," in the issue of September 23, 1848. The editor included the Aubry trail news as follows:

> Mr. Aubrey reports as water bound, at Sand Creek, Major Reynold's division of Missouri Volunteers. Major Walker's battalion, and Lieut. Love with a small number of U.S. Dragoons. There were with this party Messrs. Fisley, Allen, Carey and McCarty, traders.
>
> He passed Col. Ralls and a portion of the Missouri Volunteers at the Battle Ground, 15 miles beyond the Arkansas.
>
> Col. Easton's battalion, with the recruits under Lieut. Allen, were at Fort Mann.
>
> Gen. Price and staff were water-bound at the Pawnee Fork; also Major Donaldson's division of Illinois Volunteers, and Lieut. Cooley, of Col. Gilpin's command.
>
> At Cow Creek, he passed Capts. Cunningham and Bond's division of Illinois Volunteers, water-bound. At this place he also saw S. Ruland, of this city.
>
> He passed Col. Newby, Dr. Robinson and Lieut. Hamilton, at Willow Springs.
>
> He met Governor Lane, *en route* for Oregon, at Council Grove.
>
> Mr. Aubrey thinks that the first detachment of Gen. Price's command will reach Independence about the first of October, and the whole military force may be expected to arrive by the fifteenth.

1850 In early July of 1850, Aubry returned to Missouri after trading in New Mexico, Texas, and Chihuahua. In a full-column article on July 8, the *Daily Missouri Republican* summarized all the news brought

in by Aubry, and printed the following extracts from
his journal on the Santa Fe Trail:

> June 21. At the lower crossing of the Cimarron, Mr. A. met
> a man with the mail, also Pike, Vasquez, Hatcher, Wood, Brani-
> ford and McCarty, with 20 wagons.
>
> June 22. Below Middle Spring met Majors Morris and Gra-
> ham, Capt. Easton and several other officers and their families,
> and 100 recruits for the 3d Infantry.
>
> 23. Lower Spring of Cimarone, met Old Bob Brent, Spencer
> and lady, Kearney, Senecal, Fraser, Bianco, Mitchel, Dalton, Gui-
> terrey's son-in-law. At Sand Creek, Mrs. M. C. McKnight and
> sister, and Patterson, with 21 wagons, and Messrs. Beech and
> Estes, with 20 wagons.
>
> 25th, at the crossing of the Arkansas met Webb with 22 wag-
> ons, Vasquez, Tom McCarty and Kitchen, with 20 wagons, and
> Ewing with 100 cows.
>
> 26th – Met a large party of Indians. They were quite friendly,
> being satisfied that the strength of Mr. Aubry's party was too
> much for them.
>
> 27th, saw on the lower road six trains of wagons. On this day
> a war party of Comanche and Kiowa Indians numbering 150
> warriors, crossed the Arkansas, on their way to fight the Pawnees.
>
> 28th – Met Sims, with 30 wagons, water bound at the Pawnee
> Fork.
>
> 29th – A band of Osages made a bold attempt to run off a por-
> tion of Mr. A.'s animals. A few shots were fired by his guards,
> when the Osages retreated.
>
> 30 – At Chavis' Creek, met Davy, with 24 wagons, for Chi-
> huahua.
>
> July 3d, at 110, met a Quarter Master's train, of 40 wagons.

1850 So far no journals have been discovered of
Aubry's routes in Texas and Chihuahua, although he
did comment on several occasions to editors on trail
conditions. The following brief letter appeared in the
Daily Missouri Republican of December 14, 1850:

San Antonio, Texas, Nov. 23, 1850.

The Indians often come within a few miles of this place, to remind the citizens that they are still in the wild country. Several depredations have recently been committed within fifteen miles of this place.

It is likely that the subsistence stores for the posts at El Paso, Dona Ana, and all those south of the Jornado del Muerto, will be brought from Missouri. The freight would cost the Government at least fifty per cent less. With the Government it is a question of dollars and cents, and there is no doubt that the Quartermaster General will discover that the Missouri route is the best, safest, and cheapest.

F. X. A.

1851 On his spring, 1851, trip from Santa Fe to Independence, Aubry kept a journal. The "interesting intelligence," brought by the man "whose expeditious trips across the plains have become celebrated," appeared in the *Daily Missouri Republican,* May 19, 1851. The newspaper extracted and summarized the journal as follows:

He left Santa Fe on the 23d April. The Commissioners to locate the boundary between Mexico and the United States were on the Rio Grande, below Dona Ana, and had decided to place the corner stone six or seven miles below Dona Ana.

The troops in New Mexico are dying of the scurvy, for want of exercise. Up to the present time, it has been the policy not to permit them to follow or punish the Indians, when they have killed our citizens and it was in their power to chastize them. It is added that the young officers and soldiers are permitted to lead a life which is ruinous to their health, and many have died. The Apaches, who killed White and Flourney, have violated the treaty which they made only a month or two ago. They went to Barclay's Fort, ran off fourteen head of beef cattle, and committed other depredations. At that time the Apaches were encamped a short distance from the Fort; an express was sent to

Lt. Col. Alexander, to inform him of the facts. Orders were immediately sent to San Miguel for a company of United States Dragoons, under command of Lt. Chapman. They reached Los Vegas in a dark night, and in passing over the mountains Lt. Chapman was thrown from his horse and severely injured. On reaching Los Vegas, the company was ordered to be stationed around the town, and this is the extent of the punishment awarded for the violation of the treaty.

Gov. Calhoun had so far given entire satisfaction to the people of New Mexico, and it was the opinion that he would continue to do so.

The mail from the United States was met at Pecos church. It contained information of the rejection of the nomination of Hugh N. Smith as Secretary of the Territory – a matter which will be received with regret by the people of New Mexico, with whom Mr. Smith had a larger popularity than any other American.

Separate meetings had nominated Capt. A. W. Reynolds and Maj. R. H. Weightman as candidates for Delegate in Congress. There was a good deal of excitement, and a vast deal of log rolling, throughout the Territory, on the subject.

Gov. Calhoun has issued his proclamation appointing the 19th inst. for the election of members of the Legislature. A large meeting of citizens was held in Santa Fe on the 22d, Robert Brent in the chair, at which candidates for the Legislature were nominated. It is stated that the priests in the country were candidates for the Legislature, and they were sure of being elected.

There were three inches of snow in Santa Fe when Mr. Aubry left.

On the 29th, the company passed five trains of wagons belonging to Mexicans: they are on their way to Missouri, to purchase goods.

On the same day they left the Santa Fe road, two miles from Cold Spring, and traveled eight miles by compass crossing the Cimarone, with the view of finding a better road, they obtained grass, wood and water in abundance. On the 1st, the party traveled until midnight – made 35 miles – saw no water, wood nor grass for twenty-four hours. They traveled during the day on high table land, just as level as a billiard table, except when they had to go a mile out of their way to cross a canon. It was explored three or four miles, and found to be from three to four hundred feet deep, and thirty to sixty yards wide. They had now only one gallon of water in camp, and were satisfied that no route could be obtained, and they determined to make for the Arkansas as fast as possible.

On the 3d they arrived at the river, their animals having been two days without water. The last day the party had no water to drink, and they traveled through sand and a hot sun, and had to drink the blood of the Antelope.

On the 4th they passed 30 lodges of Cheyenne Indians, on their way to Ft. Mackay. Next day, at Ft. Mackay, they saw five tribes of Indians assembled there to make peace with Col. Hoffman. The tribes were the Comanches, Cheyennes, Arrapahoes, Kiowas and Apaches of the Plains. Both sides of the river were crowded with lodges for at least fifteen miles. The principal chiefs of each tribe were sitting in Council in Col. Hoffman's tent, and the ceremony of smoking the pipe of peace had taken place. Col. Hoffman had acted with prudence and care, and the Indians appeared to be well satisfied with him. It is probable, that the Cheyennes and Arrapahoes will respect the treaty – the others will not.

On the 7th, they met the United States mail in charge of Ellson, at Big Owl Creek. On the 10th, they passed Young and party at Lost Spring. Next day, they met John Simms, with Messervy's train of sixty wagons, at Bridge Creek. At 110, they met W. S. Messervy on his return to New Mexico. Saw Spalding, of Los Vegas, on his way to New Mexico, with a drove of cows. Beck & Brent's train of twenty-five wagons at Willow Point, and some wagons whose owners were not known.

On the 12th, Mr. Aubrey arrived at Independence in nineteen days from Santa Fe – traveling from Cotton Wood to Independence in two days and one hour – a distance of two hundred miles.

We shall give extracts from the papers tomorrow. We observe that Gov. Calhoun has appointed D. V. Whiting to be Acting Secretary of the Territory, in place of Hugh N. Smith, resigned.

1851   This account was sent in from Independence on

October 11 and appeared in the *Daily Missouri Republican* of October 13. The following items were extracted from Aubry's journal:

> The party consisted of sixty-two men, thirty wagons, and three hundred mules. Messrs. Messervy, Delemater, Spencer, Delamie, and Morely, were of the party; also, Dr. Mallory, Simms, Hoven and Ranney, gentlemen connected with the boundary commission. The health of New Mexico is good.
>
> The corn crop on the Rio Abajo is excellent – in other parts of the Territory, a failure.
>
> Col. Sumner was heard of near Lami, going on well.
>
> Maj. R. W. Weightman is elected delegate to the next Congress, by a majority of 400 to 500.
>
> W. S. Allen, Secretary of the Territory, is discharging the duties of his office very acceptably to the people.
>
> Bands of Americans, supposed to be discharged government hands, disguised as Indians, are engaged in frequent depredations.
>
> Memorandum of parties met on the way: At Los Vegas, Grotman's train, Sept. 15th; U.S. mail, Sept. 21st, at Point of Rocks; Hasten and party the same day. October 6th, McCauslin's train at Little Arkansas; Chiles' train at Turkey Creek, also Mason and Dyon's train. Jones & Russell's, and U.S. mail at Cotton Wood.
>
> Mr. Aubrey and party have traveled a new route, diverging from the old route at Cold Spring, and thence to the Arkansas, from ten to forty degrees east of north – finding an excellent wagon road, well supplied with water and grass, and avoiding the Jornada and Cimarone trail altogether. It will prove a great advantage to traveling trains.
>
> Mr. Aubrey, on his famous mare Dolly, came in advance from Cotton Wood, at the rate of 100 miles per day.

1852   This account, which appeared in the *Daily Missouri Republican* of August 31, 1852, was most likely a combination of extracts from an Aubry journal, plus an interview:

Mr. F. X. Aubry, the fleet traveler of the Prairie, arrived in this city last night from Santa Fe, in good health. He left Santa Fe on the 31st of July, and arrived at Independence on the 25th inst. – making the trip in twenty-five days. The party consisted of fifty men, twelve wagons, two carriages and two hundred and fifty mules. Maj. Van Horn, of the Army, and Messrs. Kearney and Dyer were of the party. The sum of $25,000 in specie, and $30,000 in drafts, was also brought in.

Mrs. and Miss King, of Georgia, we believe, died on the Arkansas in the month of July. Mr. Chouteau's pleasure party was on the Arkansas – all in good health.

Mr. Aubry saw three hundred lodges of Comanches and Kiowas on Rabbit Ear Creek.

Capt. Buckner and Lieut. Woodruff, were to leave Fort Atkinson on the 25th for the States. Mr. Chouteau's party would return with them. Lieut. Woodruff has explored the country North and South of the Arkansas river, and it is understood that he has reported in favor of a route along the Pawnee Fork and Buckner's Branch, to intersect the road made by Aubry from Cold Spring to the Arkansas.

Governor Lane arrived at Fort Atkinson on the 15th instant.

Bishop Lemay's party was met at Cottonwood, and Major Fitzpatrick, with Lieut. Heath of the army, at Lost Spring. They were making forced marches in order to deliver the presents which they had in charge to the Comanches, at an early day. Mr. W. S. Stone was on the Arkansas, Beck at Diamond Spring and Major and lady at 110.

Major Backus, Major Graham, and lady, Dr. M. Dougall, Capt. Buford, Mrs. Howe, Mr. West and lady, and many others, were to leave Fort Union for the States on the 20th inst.

Mr. Aubry learned from Maj. Van Horn, that about the 1st July eight Apache Indians made an attack upon fifteen Mexicans in the *Jornada del Muerto,* . . . without receiving any injury. They took from them twenty oxen. The Indians started off, and at a few miles distance, again come up with them, when the Mexicans bought the same oxen from them, giving in exchange one horse and three mules, and then made peace with them.

Bibliography

Bibliography

Manuscript material for Aubry is rich, but thin. I have followed his career mostly through the newspapers of Saint Louis and Santa Fe, although for certain events newspapers in cities such as Sacramento, Los Angeles, and San Francisco were helpful. The published accounts on Aubry in the twentieth century are usually unreliable, given to exaggeration, trumped up conversations, and so forth. This is especially true for romantic accounts in such magazines as *Old West, Desert Magazine, True West,* and others. However, the material in historical journals was useful, especially the work of Ralph Bieber, Walker Wyman, and Leo Oliva.

Most of my work with manuscripts was at the Huntington Library, although I did have the opportunity to use fine collections at the Bancroft Library, the Missouri Historical Society, and the State Records Center in Santa Fe. Most books, government documents, and other published material were from the Huntington Library. Of the several dozen newspapers used in this study, most were obtained on inter-library loan from the State Historical Society of Missouri and the Museum of New Mexico.

MANUSCRIPTS

Albuquerque, N.Mex., Univ. of N.M: F. D. Reeve Papers; Michael
Steck Papers

Austin, Texas State Lby: Santa Fe Papers

Berkeley, Bancroft Lby., Univ. of Calif: Elias Brevoort Papers; Santa
Fe Misc. Papers

Colorado Springs, Pioneer Museum: Early Far-West Notebooks

Denver, Pub. Lby; Western History Dept: William Baskerville
Papers

Las Vegas, N.Mex., Highlands Univ: Arrott Coll.

Quebec, Archives Nationales: Family History Section

Saint Louis, Missouri Hist. Soc: Solomon Sublette Papers; Turley
Papers

Saint Louis, Saint Louis Univ., Pius XII Lby: Student Enrollment
and Residence files

San Marino, Calif., Huntington Lby: William Ritch Papers; Russell, Majors & Waddell Papers

Santa Fe, County Courthouse: Records of First Judicial Dist.; Records of Rio Ariva; Records of U.S. District Court

Santa Fe, State Records Center: Benjamin Read Coll.; Arch. of the
Archdiocese of Santa Fe (microfilm)

Trois-Rivières, Quebec, Séminaire Saint-Joseph: Saint-Justin Parish
Records; Aubry Family Coll.

Tucson, Arizona Hist. Soc. Lby: Heyden File (contains an Aubry
section)

Washington, D.c., Nat. Arch: Record Group 98 (army trail explorations); Office of Indian Affairs, Letters Received, N.Mex. Superintendency, 1851-53

GOVERNMENT PUBLICATIONS

Mr. Gwin of California, Speeches of . . . *Delivered in the
Senate* . . . *Dec. 12, 1853.* Wash: Congressional Globe, 1853
(Aubrey's 1853 journal)

Rapport de l'Archiviste de la Province de Québec, 1951-53. Quebec:
Provincial Arch., 1954 (Aubry family history)

*Report of Cases Argued and Determined in the Supreme Court, Ter-
ritory of New Mexico from January Term, 1852, to January Term,
1879.* Chicago: Callaghan & Co., 1911 (Aubry v. Nangle)

U.S., House, Exec. Doc. 1, *Annual Report, Secretary of War,* 30th Cong., 2d sess. (1848-49)

U.S., House, Exec. Doc. 17, *California and New Mexico: Message from the President of the United States,* 31st Cong., 1st sess. (1850) (map, assistance to Aubry from the 1st Dragoons)

U.S., Senate, Exec. Doc. 26, *Report on Affairs Relating to New Mexico,* 31st Cong., 2d sess. (1850)

U.S., Senate, Exec. Doc. 1, *Annual Report, Secretary of War,* 32nd Cong., 1st sess. (1851)

U.S., Senate, Exec. Doc. 18, *Report of the Secretary of War Showing Contracts Made . . . 1852,* 32nd Cong., 2d sess. (1852)

U.S., Senate, Exec. Doc. 78, *Reports of Explorations and Surveys to Ascertain the Most Practicable and Economic Route for a Railroad from the Mississippi River to the Pacific Ocean,* 33rd Cong., 2d sess., 13 vols., 1853-56 (known as *Pacific Railroad Reports*)

U.S., Senate, Exec. Doc. 1, *Annual Report, Commissioner of Indian Affairs,* 37th Cong., 2d sess. (1862) (Henry Mercure)

Hon. Richard H. Weightman of New Mexico, Speeches of . . . Wash: Congressional Globe, 1852

BOOKS AND ARTICLES

Abel, Annie H. *Official Correspondence of James S. Calhoun.* Wash: Gov. Pntg. Office, 1915

Adams, Ramon F. "The Cowman's Code of Ethics," *Westerner's Brand Book, 1949* Denver: Denver Posse, 1950, pp. 149-64

Allison, W.H.H. "Colonel Francisco Perea," *Old Santa Fe,* 1 (Oct. 1913), 210-22

Aubry, F.X. "Diary of a Journey Through Arizona," (1853), *Railroad Record,* Mar. 25, 1856, offprint, Nat. Hist. Mus., Los Angeles

Bieber, Ralph P. (ed.) "Letters of James and Robert Aull," *Missouri Hist. Soc. Coll.,* v (1927-28), 267-310

Barry, Louise. *The Beginning of the West: Annals of the Kansas Gateway to the American West, 1540-1854.* Topeka: Kan. St. Hist. Soc., 1973

Barry, Louise. "Fort Aubrey," *Kan. Hist. Quar.,* xxxix (Summer 1973), 188-99

Bender, A.B. "Opening Routes across West Texas, 1848-1850," *Southwestern Hist. Quar.,* xxxvii (Oct. 1933), 116-35

Bennett, James A. *Forts and Forays: A Dragoon in New Mexico, 1850-1856,* ed. by Charles E. Brooks and Frank D. Reeve. Albuquerque: Univ. of N.Mex. Press., 1948

Bernard, William R. "Westport and the Santa Fe Trade," *Trans. of the Kan. State Hist. Soc.,* IX (1905-06), 552-78

Bieber, Ralph P. (ed.). *Exploring Southwestern Trails, 1846-1854.* Glendale: Arthur H. Clark Co., 1938. (Aubry's 1853 and 1854 journals)

Bieber, Ralph P. "Some Aspects of the Santa Fe Trail," *Chronicles of Oklahoma,* II (Mar. 1924), 1-8

Billington, Ray Allen. *The Far Western Frontier, 1830-1860.* New York: Harper & Row, 1956

Billington, Ray Allen. *Westward Expansion: History of the American Frontier.* New York: Macmillan Co., 1950

Bloom, Lansing B. (ed.). "From Lewisburg (Pa.) to California in 1849, (Notes from the Diary of William H. Chamberlain)," *N.Mex. Hist. Rev.,* XX (Jan. 1945), 14-57

Bloom, Lansing B. (ed.). "Historical Society Minutes, 1854-1863," *N.Mex. Hist. Rev.,* XVIII (July 1943), 247-311

Bott, Emily Ann O'Neill. "Joseph Murphy's Contribution to the Development of the West," *Missouri Hist. Rev.,* XLVII (Oct. 1952), 18-28

Brandes, Ray. "Guide to the Landmarks of Tucson," *Arizoniana,* III (Summer 1962), 27-38

Brayer, Garnet. (ed.). *Land of Enchantment: Memoirs of Marian Russell Along the Santa Fe Trail.* Evanston: Branding Iron Press, 1954

Brewerton, George D. "In the Buffalo Country," *Harper's New Monthly Mag.,* XXV (Aug. 1862), 447-66

Brewerton, George Douglas. *Overland with Kit Carson.* New York: Coward-McCann, 1930. (Brewerton's 1848 account)

Brewerton, George Douglas. *Wars of the Western Border.* New York: Derby & Jackson, 1859

Brown, Harry E. *The Medical Department of the United States Army from 1775 to 1873.* Wash: Surgeon General's Office, 1873

Browne, J. Ross. *Adventures in the Apache Country: A Tour Through Arizona and Sonora.* New York: Harper & Bros., 1869

Bundschu, Henry A. "Francis Xavier Aubry," *Pacific Historian,* v (Aug. 1961), 116-23

Calvin, Ross. "Westward Empire," *N.Mex. Mag.,* xxiv (July 1946), 14-15, 41-45

Campagna, F. Dominique. *Repertoire des Mariages de Maskinongé, 1728-1966.* Cap-de-la-Madeleine, Quebec: the author, 1966

Case, Theo. S. (ed.). *History of Kansas City, Missouri.* New York: D. Mason, Publ., 1888

Chapman, Arthur. *The Pony Express.* New York: G. P. Putnam's Sons, 1932

Chaput, Donald. "Babes in Arms," *Journal of Ariz. Hist.,* xiii (Autumn 1972), 197-204

Cohen, Aaron. (ed.). *The Santa Fe Trail: People & Places: A Catalogue of Books and Pamphlets.* Scottsdale, Ariz: Guidon Books, 1973

Conkling, Roscoe P. and Margaret. *The Butterfield Overland Mail Company.* Glendale: Arthur H. Clark Co., 1947

Connelley, William E. *Doniphan's Expedition and the Conquest of New Mexico and California.* Topeka: the Author, 1907

Conrad, Howard L. (ed.). *Encyclopedia of the History of Missouri.* New York: Southern History Co., 1901

Dains, Mary K. "Steamboats of the 1850's-1860's: A Pictorial History," *Missouri Hist. Rev.,* lxvii (Jan. 1973), 265-82

Darton, N.H. *Guidebook of the Western United States: Part C. The Santa Fe Route.* Wash: Gov. Pntg. Office, 1915

Davis, W.W.H. *El Gringo; or, New Mexico and Her People.* New York: Harper & Row, 1857

Defouri, James H. *Historical Sketch of the Catholic Church in New Mexico.* San Francisco: McCormick Bros., 1887

DeVoto, Bernard. *The Year of Decision: 1846.* Boston: Little, Brown & Co., 1943

Dick, Everett. *Vanguards of the Frontier.* Lincoln: Univ. of Neb. Press, 1941

Dobie, J. Frank. "The Saga of the Saddle," *Southwest Review,* xiii (Jan. 1928), 127-42

Drouin, Gabriel. (ed.). *Dictionnaire National des Canadiens Français.* Montreal: Institut Drouin, 1958

Drumm, Stella M. (ed.). *Down the Santa Fe Trail and into Mexico: Diary of Susan Shelby Magoffin, 1846-1847.* New Haven: Yale Univ. Press, 1926

Duffus, R.L. *The Santa Fe Trail.* New York: Tudor Publ. Co., 1930

Encyclopedia of the History of St. Louis. New York: Southern History Co., 1899

Estergreen, M. Morgan. *Kit Carson: A Portrait in Courage.* Norman: Univ. of Okla. Press, 1962

"Famous Rides of the West," *New York Times Mag.,* Apr. 1, 1928, p. 21

Farish, Thomas Edwin. *History of Arizona.* Phoenix: n.n., 1915

Foreman, Grant. *A Pathfinder in the Southwest* (Lt. A. W. Whipple). Norman: Univ. of Okla. Press, 1941

Frazer, Robert. *Forts of the West.* Norman: Univ. of Okla. Press, 1965

Fugate, Francis L. "Francis X. Aubry: Skimmer of the Plains," *New Mexico Sun Trails,* VIII (Jan.-Feb. 1955), 6-9

Ganaway, Loomis Morton. *New Mexico and the Sectional Controversy, 1846-1861.* Albuquerque: Univ. of N.Mex. Press, 1944

Garrard, Lewis H. *Wah-to-yah and the Taos Trail.* Norman: Univ. of Okla. Press, 1962

Gibson, George Rutledge. *Journal of a Soldier under Kearny and Doniphan, 1846-1847,* ed. by Ralph P. Bieber. Glendale: Arthur H. Clark Co., 1935

Greene, J. Evarts. *The Santa Fe Trade: Its Route and Character.* Worcester, Mass: Press of Chas. Hamilton, 1893

Greene, Max. *The Kanzas Region.* New York: Fowler & Well, 1856

Gregg, Josiah. *The Commerce of the Prairies,* ed. by Milo Quaife. Lincoln: Univ. of Neb. Press, 1967

Hafen, LeRoy R. (ed.). *Fremont's Fourth Expedition: The Disaster of 1848-1849.* Glendale: Arthur H. Clark Co., 1960. (includes diary of Richard Kern)

Hafen, LeRoy R. (ed.). *The Mountain Men and the Fur Trade of the Far West.* Glendale: Arthur H. Clark Co., 1965-1973

Hafen, LeRoy. *The Overland Mail.* Cleveland: Arthur H. Clark Co., 1926

Heitman, Francis B. *Historical Register and Dictionary of the United States Army.* Wash: Gov. Pntg. Office, 1903

History of the State of Kansas. Chicago: A. T. Andreas, 1883

Holden, W.C. "Frontier Defense, 1846-1860," *West Texas Hist. Assoc. Year Book,* VI (1930), 35-65

Hough, John. "Early Western Experiences," *Colorado Mag.,* XVII (May 1940), 101-12

Howlett, William. *Life of Bishop Machebeuf.* Pueblo, Colo: Franklin Press, 1908

Hunt, Aurora. *Kirby Benedict: Frontier Federal Judge.* Glendale: Arthur H. Clark Co., 1961

Jones, Hester. "The Spiegelbergs and Early Trade in New Mexico," *El Palacio,* XXXVIII (Apr. 1935), 81-89

Jones, J. Robert. "The President (Mercure) in Santa Fe." *N.Mex. Mag.,* XXIX (Jan. 1951), 17

Jordan, Philip D. *Frontier Law and Order.* Lincoln: Univ. of Neb. Press, 1970

Karnes, Thomas L. *William Gilpin, Western Nationalist.* Austin: Univ. of Tex. Press, 1970

Keleher, William A. *Turmoil in New Mexico, 1846-1868.* Santa Fe: Rydal Press, 1952

Kroeber, A.L. *Handbook of the Indians of California.* Wash: Gov. Pntg. Office, 1925

Kroeber, A.L. "Yuman Tribes of the Lower Colorado," *Univ. of Calif. Publications in Archaeology and Ethnology,* XVI (1920), 475-85

"La Famille Aubrenan ou Aubry," *Bulletin des Recherches Historiques,* XI (Nov. 1934), 641-44

Lamb's Biographical Dictionary of the United States. Boston: James H. Lamb Co., 1900

Lane, William Carr. "Letters of, 1852-1854," ed. by Ralph P. Bieber. *N.Mex. Hist. Rev.,* III (Apr. 1928), 179-203

Lane, William Carr. "Diary," ed. by William G. B. Carson. *N.Mex. Hist. Rev.* XXXIX (Oct. 1964), 274-332

Lavender, David. *Bent's Fort.* Garden City: Doubleday & Co., 1954

Lesley, Lewis Burt. (ed.). *Uncle Sam's Camels.* Cambridge: Harvard Univ. Press, 1929. (includes reports of Edward F. Beale)

Lockwood, Frank C. "Arizona Pioneers: Francois Xavier Aubrey," *Ariz. Hist. Rev.,* v (Jan. 1933), 327-32

Lockwood, Frank C. "He Rode the Wilderness Trail," *Desert Magazine,* ix (Mar. 1946), 28-30

Long, Margaret. *The Santa Fe Trail.* Denver: n.n., 1954

Lowe, Percival. *Five Years a Dragoon (1849-54), and other Adventures on the Great Plains,* ed. by Don Russell. Norman: Univ. of Okla. Press, 1965

Malchelosse, Gérard. "A Propos de nos Origines," *Cahier des Dix,* xii (1947), 231-63

Majors, Alexander. *Seventy Years on the Frontier.* Columbus, Ohio: College Book Co., 1950

Marcou, Jules. *Geology of North America.* Zurich: Zurcher & Furrer, 1858

Marcy, Randolph. *The Prairie Traveler.* New York: Harper & Bros., 1859

Miner, H. Craig. *The St. Louis-San Francisco Transcontinental Railroad: The Thirty-fifth Parallel Project, 1853-1890.* Lawrence: Univ. Press of Kan., 1972

Montague's Illinois and Missouri State Directory, 1854-5. St. Louis: Montague, 1854

Moorhead, Max L. *New Mexico's Royal Road.* Norman: Univ. of Okla. Press, 1958

Morice, A.G. *Dictionnaire Historique des Canadiens de l'Ouest.* Quebec: J. P. Garneau, 1908

Myers, John Myers. *The Death of the Bravos.* Boston: Little, Brown & Co., 1962

Oliva, Leo E. "The Aubry Route of the Santa Fe Trail," *Kan. Quar.,* v (Spring 1973), 18-29

Pacific Railroad Reports: *see* Government Publications

Perrigo, Lynn I. *Texas and our Spanish Southwest.* Dallas: Banks Upshaw & Co., 1960

Peterson, Harold L. *American Knives: The First History and Collectors Guide.* New York: Chas. Scribner's Sons, 1958

Plante, Hermann. *Saint-Justin, foyer de sérénité rurale.* Trois-Rivières: Pages Trifluviènnes, Série A., No. 19, 1937

Poldervaart, Arie W. *Black-robed Justice.* Santa Fe: Hist. Soc. of N.Mex., 1948

Reed, Bill. "Frontier Adventurer," *N.Mex. Mag.,* xxix (July 1931), 26, 43-45

Riddle, Kenyon. *Records and Maps of the Old Santa Fe Trail.* Raton, N.Mex: Raton Daily Range, 1949

Riordan, Marguerite. "Freighter on Horseback," *The Cattleman* (Jan. 1953), pp. 102-07

Rittenhouse, Jack D. *The Santa Fe Trail: A Historical Bibliography.* Albuquerque: Univ. of N.Mex. Press, 1971

Root, Frank A., and Connelley, William E. *The Overland Stage to California.* Columbus, Ohio: Long's College Book Co., 1950

Rosa, Joseph G. *The Gunfighter: Man or Myth?* Norman: Univ. of Okla. Press, 1969

Roy, Pierre-Georges. *Inventaire des Contrats de Mariage du Régime Français.* 6 vols. Quebec: Arch. de Quebec, 1937. (Aubry data in Vol. i)

Russell, Marian. "Memoirs of   .   ." *Colorado Mag.,* xx (1943), 81-95, 140-54, 181-96, 226-38; xxi (1944), 29-37, 62-74, 101-12

Ruxton, George Frederick. *Wild Life in the Rocky Mountains,* ed. by Horace Kephart. New York: Macmillan Co., 1937

S & D Reflector (Marietta, Ohio), x (Sept. 1973), 22. (Comments on steamer Aubrey)

Sabin, Edwin L. *Kit Carson Days, 1809-1868.* New York: Press of the Pioneers, 1935

Saint Louis Directory, 1842. St. Louis: Chambers & Knapp, 1842

Saint Louis Directory, 1854-5. St. Louis: Chambers & Knapp, 1854

Schoolcraft, Henry. *Information Respecting the History Condition and Prospects of the Indian Tribes of the United States.* Phila: J. B. Lippencott & Co., 1855. (Gov. Lane on Aubry in Vol. v)

Schrantz, Ward L. "The Battle of Carthage," *Missouri Hist. Rev.,* xxxi (Jan. 1937), 140-49

Settle, Raymond. "Origin of the Pony Express," *Bull. of the Missouri Hist. Soc.,* xvi (Apr. 1960), 199-212

Settle, Raymond W., and Settle, Mary Lund. *Saddles and Spurs: The Pony Express Saga.* Harrisburg, Pa: Stackpole Co., 1955

Sheldon, Roger. "Plainsman in a Hurry," *Old West,* ii (Winter 1965), 43, 68

Memoirs of General William T. Sherman. New York: D. Appleton & Co., 1875

Smart, Charles. "Notes on the 'Tonto' Apaches," *Annual Rep., Smithsonian Inst., 1867,* pp. 417-19

Smith, Waddell. *The Story of the Pony Express.* San Rafael, Calif: Pony Express Gallery, 1964

Stanley, F. *Giant in Lilliput: Story of Donaciano Vigil.* Pampa, Tex: Pampa Book Shop, 1963

Stewart, Kenneth M. "Mohave Warfare," *Southwestern Jour. of Anth.,* III (Autumn 1947), 257-78

Sulte, Benjamin. "F.-X. Aubry," *Bulletin des Recherches Historiques,* xv (Nov. 1909), 351-52

Sulte, Benjamin. "Les Forges Saint-Maurice," *Mélanges Historiques,* VI (1920), 85-110

Tassé, Joseph. "F.-X. Aubry," *Les Canadiens de l'Ouest.* Montreal: Cie. d'Imprimerie Canadienne, 1878, II, pp. 179-227

Taylor, Morris F. *First Mail West: Stagecoach Lines on the Santa Fe Trail.* Albuquerque: Univ. of N.Mex. Press, 1971

Theobald, John and Lillian. *Arizona Territory Post Offices.* Phoenix: Ariz. Hist. Foundation, 1961

Towne, Charles Wayland, and Wentworth, Edward Norris. *Shepherd's Empire.* Norman: Univ. of Okla. Press, 1945

Twitchell, Ralph Emerson. *The History of the Military Occupation of New Mexico from 1846 to 1851.* Denver: Smith-Brooks Co., 1909

Twitchell, Ralph Emerson. "Kirby Benedict," *Old Santa Fe,* I (July 1913), 50-92

Twitchell, Ralph Emerson. *The Leading Facts of New Mexican History.* Cedar Rapids, Iowa: Torch Press, 1912

Twitchell, Ralph Emerson. *Old Santa Fe.* Santa Fe: New Mexico Pub. Corp., 1925

Upham, Charles W. *Life, Explorations and Public Services of John Charles Fremont.* Boston: Ticknor & Fields, 1856

Visscher, William Lightfoot. *The Pony Express.* Chicago: Rand, McNally, 1908

Waldo, William. "Recollections of a Septuagenarian," *Glimpses of the Past,* v (Apr.-June 1938), 59-94

Walker, Henry Pickering. *The Wagonmasters: High Plains Freighting from the Earliest Days of the Santa Fe Trail to 1880.* Norman: Univ. of Okla. Press, 1966

Walter, Paul A.F.; Clancy, Frank W.; and Otero, M.A. *Colonel José Francisco Chaves, 1833-1924*. Santa Fe: Hist. Soc. of N.Mex., 1926

Webb, James Josiah. *Adventures in the Santa Fe Trade, 1844-1847*, ed. by Ralph P. Bieber. Glendale: Arthur H. Clark Co., 1931

Bieber, Ralph P. (ed.). "The Papers of James J. Webb, Santa Fe Merchant," *Wash. Univ. Studies,* Vol. XI Humanistic Ser. #2 (1924), 255-305

Wentworth, Edward N. "Meat in the Diet of Westward Explorers and Emigrants," *Mid-America,* XXIX (Apr. 1947), 75-91

Wetmore, Alphonso. *Gazetteer of the State of Missouri*. St. Louis: C. Keemle, 1837

Wilson, Richard L. *Short Ravelings from a Long Yarn . . . of the Santa Fe Trail*. Chicago: Geer & Wilson, 1847

Wood, Dean Earl. *The Old Santa Fe Trail from the Missouri River*. Kansas City: E. L. Mendenhall, Inc., 1955

Wyllys, Rufus. *Arizona: History of a Frontier State*. Phoenix: Hobson & Herr, 1950

Wyman, Walker D. "F. X. Aubry: Santa Fe Freighter, Pathfinder, and Explorer," *N.Mex. Hist. Rev.,* VII (Jan. 1932), 1-31. (includes Aubry's 1853 and 1854 journals)

Wyman, Walker. "Freighting: A Big Business on the Santa Fe Trail," *Kan. Hist. Quar.,* I (1931-32), 17-27

Wyman, Walker. "The Military Phase of Santa Fe Freighting, 1846-1865," *Kan. Hist. Quar.,* I (1931-32), 417-28

NEWSPAPERS

Appleton City Journal (Mo.), 1902
Independence Examiner, 1940
Kansas City Globe, 1890
Kansas City Post, 1916
Kansas City Times, 1964
Los Angeles *Southern Californian,* 1854-55
Los Angeles Star, 1853-54
Montreal Gazette, 1854
Montreal *La Minerve,* 1854
New York Daily Tribune, 1849-54
New York Herald, 1848

New York Times, 1854
New York Weekly Tribune, 1848
Niles' National Register, 1846-48
Odessa Democrat (Missouri), 1917, 1919
Pittsburgh Dispatch, 1853
Prescott *Arizona Enterprise,* 1878
Prescott *Arizona Miner,* 1866
Prescott *Morning Courier,* 1888
Quebec *Le Canadien,* 1854
Sacramento Union, 1853-54
St. Louis *Daily Missouri Democrat,* 1854
St. Louis *Daily Missouri Republican,* 1846-54
St. Louis *Daily Reveille,* 1848-50
St. Louis *Daily Union,* 1848, 1850
St. Louis Globe, 1906
St. Louis *Revue de l'Ouest,* 1854
St. Louis *Weekly Reveille,* 1849-50
San Francisco *California Farmer,* 1860
San Francisco *Daily Alta California,* 1849-54
Santa Fe *New Mexican,* 1849-72 (or, *El Nuevo Mejicano*)
Santa Fe Republican, 1847-48 (or, *El Republicano*)
Santa Fe Weekly Gazette, 1853-56
Sault Ste. Marie *Lake Superior Journal,* 1854
Tucson *Citizen,* 1873

MISCELLANEOUS

Brown, William. "The Santa Fe Trail," a mimeographed publication of the U.S. Dept. of the Int., National Park Service, 1963

Gingras, Raymond. Letter of Aug. 8, 1973, regarding Aubry ancestry; also other biographical information from the holdings of the Nat. Arch. of Quebec

Plante, Clément. Letter of Dec. 12, 1971, containing maps, photos, and documents relating to the Aubry land in St-Justin, Quebec

Plante, Fr. Hermann. Letter of Oct. 14, 1971, regarding Aubry ancestry (Fr. Plante is archivist, Séminaire St-Joseph, Trois-Rivières)

Utley, Robert M. "Fort Union and the Santa Fe Trail," a mimeographed publication of the U.S. Dept. of the Int., National Park Service, 1959

Index

Index

F   Chaput, Donald.
786   François X. Aubry : trader, trailmaker and
A892   voyageur in the Southwest, 1846-1854 / by Donald
C46   Chaput.   Glendale, Calif., A.H. Clark Co., 1975.
              249p. illus., maps (1 fold. col.) 23cm.
           (Western frontiersman series, 16)
   319392
              Bibliography: p.[225]-236.
              Includes index.

1.Aubry, François Xavier, 1824-1854.   2.Santa Fe Trail.
I.Title.   II.Series.